15 MINUTE
SPANISH
LEARN IN JUST 12 WEEKS

ANA BREMÓN

DK | Penguin Random House

Senior Editors Angeles Gavira, Christine Stroyan
Project Art Editor Vanessa Marr
DTP Designer John Goldsmid
Jacket Design Development Manager Sophia MTT
Jacket Designer Juhi Sheth
Pre-Producer David Almond
Senior Producer Ana Vallarino
Associate Publisher Liz Wheeler
Publishing Director Jonathan Metcalf

Language content for Dorling Kindersley by g-and-w publishing.

Produced for Dorling Kindersley by Schermuly Design Co.

First published in Great Britain in 2005.
This revised edition published in 2018 by
Dorling Kindersley Limited
80 Strand, London WC2R 0RL.

Copyright © 2005, 2012, 2018 Dorling Kindersley Limited
A Penguin Random House Company

2 4 6 8 10 9 7 5 3 1
01-309303-Jan/2018

A CIP catalogue record is available for this book
from the British Library.
ISBN 978-0-2413-2737-1

Printed in China

A WORLD OF IDEAS
SEE ALL THERE IS TO K

www.dk.com

CONTENTS

How to use this book

The main part of the book is devoted to 12 themed chapters, broken down into five 15-minute daily lessons, the last of which is a revision lesson. So, in just 12 weeks you will have completed the course. A concluding reference section contains a menu guide and English-to-Spanish and Spanish-to-English dictionaries.

Warm up
Each day starts with a warm up that encourages you to recall vocabulary or phrases you have learned previously. To the right of the heading bar you will see how long you need to spend on each exercise.

Instructions
Each exercise is numbered and introduced by instructions that explain what to do. In some cases additional information is given about the language point being covered.

Cultural/Conversational tip
These panels provide additional insights into life in Spain and language usage.

How to use the flap
The book's cover flaps allow you to conceal the Spanish so that you can test whether you have remembered correctly.

Revision pages
A recap of selected elements of previous lessons helps to reinforce your knowledge.

18   WEEK 2

1 Warm up (1 minute)

Count to ten. (pp.10–11)

Remind yourself how to say "hello" and "goodbye". (pp.8–9)

Ask "Do you have a son?" (pp.14–15)

EN LA CAFETER
In the café

In a Spanish café you can get bread an your coffee in the mornings. **Churros** sticks) are a typical Spanish snack. You the counter or have waiter service at a to tip the waiter, but a few coins is usu

2 Words to remember (5 minutes)

Familiarize yourself with these words.

el té con limón *el tay kon leemon*	tea with lemon
el café descafeinado *el kafay deskafeynadoh*	decaffeinated coffee
el cortado *el kortadoh*	espresso with a bit of milk
la mermelada *lah mermeladah*	jam
la tostada con mantequilla *lah tostadah kon mantekee-yah*	toast with butter

el café solo
el kafay soloh
espresso

Cultural tip A standard coffee is small and black; if want it any other way, you'll need to specify. If you wa with milk, ask for **té con leche**. If you just ask for **té**, ye likely to get tea with lemon.

3 In conversation (4 minutes)

Buenos días. Me pone un café con leche.
bwenos deeyas. may ponay oon kafay kon lechay

¿Eso es todo?
esoh es todoh
Is that all?

¿Tiene c
tyenay cf
Do you f

36   WEEK 3

Respuestas
Answers (Cover with flap)

1 Sums
❶ dieciséis *deeythesays*
❷ treinta y nueve *traintah ee nwebay*
❸ cincuenta y tres *theenkwentah ee tres*
❹ setenta y cuatro *setentah ee kwatroh*
❺ noventa y nueve *nobentah ee nwebay*

REPASE Y REPITA
Review and repeat

1 Sums (4 minutes)

Say the answers to these sums out loud in Spanish. Then check you have remembered correctly.

❶ 10 + 6 = ?
❷ 14 + 25 = ?
❸ 66 − 13 = ?
❹ 40 + 34 = ?
❺ 90 + 9 = ?

3 Telephones (3 minutes)

What are the numbered items in Spanish?

mobile ❶

❷

❸ SIM card

telephone ❹

answering machine

❺ headphones

2 I want...
❶ Quiero *kyeeroy*
❷ quiere *kyeeray*
❸ queremos *keyremos*
❹ quieres *kyeeres*
❺ quieren *kyeeren*
❻ quiero *kyeeroh*

2 I want... (3 minutes)

Fill the gaps with the correct form of (to want).

❶ ¿____ usted un café?
❷ Ella ____ ir de vacaciones.
❸ Nosotros ____ una mesa para tres.
❹ Tú ____ una cerveza.
❺ Ellos ____ una mesa para dos.
❻ Yo ____ caramelos.

4 When? (2 minutes)

What do these sentences mean?
❶ Tengo una cita el lunes veinte de mayo.
❷ Mi cumpleaños es en septiembre.
❸ Hoy es domingo.
❹ No trabajo en agosto.

5 Time (2 minutes)

Say these times in Spanish.

4 Useful phrases (5 minutes)

Learn these phrases. Read the English under the pictures and say the phrase in Spanish as shown on the right. Then cover the Spanish with the cover flap and test yourself.

los churros
los choorros
churros

el azúcar
el ah-thookar
sugar

Me pone un café.
may ponay oon kafay

I'll have a black coffee.

¿Eso es todo?
esoh es todoh

Is that all?

Yo voy a tomar churros.
yoh boy ah tomar choorros

I'm going to have some churros.

¿Cuánto es?
kwantoh es

How much is that?

el café con leche
el kafay kon lechay
white coffee

Useful phrases
Selected phrases relevant to the topic help you speak and understand.

Sí, señor.
see, senyor

Yes, sir.

Gracias. ¿Cuánto es?
grathyas. kwantoh es

Thank you. How much is that?

Cuatro euros, por favor.
kwatroh eh-ooros, por fabor

Four euros, please.

Text styles
Distinctive text styles differentiate Spanish and English, and the pronunciation guide.

In conversation
Illustrated dialogues reflecting how vocabulary and phrases are used in everyday situations appear throughout the book.

Say it
In these exercises you are asked to apply what you have learned using different vocabulary.

6 Say it (2 minutes)

Do you go near the train station?

Do you go near the Prado?

When is the next bus to Barcelona?

Dictionary
A mini-dictionary provides ready
reference from English to Spanish and
Spanish to English for 2,500 words.

Menu guide
Use this guide
as a reference for
food terminology
and popular
Spanish dishes.

Pronunciation guide

This book teaches European Spanish, which differs in pronunciation from
the various dialects spoken in Latin America. A few Spanish sounds require
special explanation:

c   a Spanish **c** is pronounced *th* before **i** or **e** but **k** before other vowels: **cinco**
         theenkoh (*five*)
h   **h** is always silent: **hola** o-lah (*hello*)
j (g) a Spanish **j** (and **g** before **i** or **e**) is pronounced as a strong *h*, as if saying <u>hat</u>
         emphasizing the first letter
ll   pronounced *y* as in *yes*
ñ   pronounced *ny* like the sound in the middle of *canyon*
r   a Spanish **r** is trilled like a Scottish *r*, especially at the beginning of a word
         and when doubled
v   a Spanish **v** is halfway between an English *b* and *v*
z   a Spanish **z** is pronounced *th*

Spanish vowels tend to be pronounced shorter than their English equivalents:
a   as the English *father*
e   as the English *wet*
i   as the English *keep*
o   as the English *boat*
u   as the English *boot*

After each word or phrase you will find a pronunciation transcription, with
underlining showing the stress. Remember that this can only be an approximation;
there is no substitute for listening to and mimicking native speakers.

How to use the audio app

All the numbered exercises in each lesson, apart from the Warm ups at the beginning and the Say it exercises at the end, have recorded audio, available via a free app. The app also includes a function to record yourself and listen to yourself alongside native speakers.

To start using the audio with the book, first download the **DK 15 Minute Language Course** app on your smart-phone or tablet from the App Store or Google Play. Open the app and scan the QR code on the back of this book to add it to your Library. As soon as the QR code is recognized, the audio will download.

There are two ways in which you can use the audio. The first is to read through your 15-minute lessons using the book only, and then go back and work with the audio and the book together, repeating the text in the gaps provided and then recording yourself. Or you can combine the book and the audio right from the beginning, pausing the app to read the instructions on the page as you need to. Try to say the words aloud, and practise enunciating properly. Detailed instructions on how to use the app are available from the menu bar in the app.

Remember that repetition is vital to language learning. The more often you listen to a conversation or repeat an oral exercise, the more the language will sink in.

Menu, Help/How to Use, Your Library

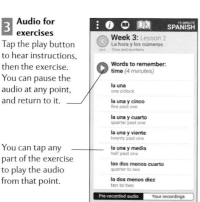

1 Getting started
The list of weeks will open when the audio has been downloaded. From here you can tap into each week's lessons.

When all the lessons in a week have been completed, the week button will be filled with colour and show a check mark, so you can track your progress.

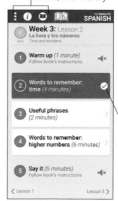

2 Lessons week by week
Each numbered exercise in a lesson is listed in the app as it appears in the book. Tap on an exercise to start.

A check mark indicates when an exercise has been completed.

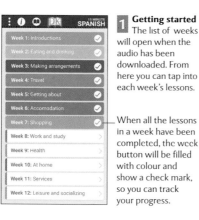

3 Audio for exercises
Tap the play button to hear instructions, then the exercise. You can pause the audio at any point, and return to it.

You can tap any part of the exercise to play the audio from that point.

4 Record yourself
When you are in the *Your recordings* screen, you can record yourself reading the words or participating in the conversations with native speakers, then listen back (and rerecord if desired).

Add recording

Play recording

HOLA
Hello

Warm up (1 minute)

The Warm Up appears at the beginning of each lesson. It will remind you of what you have already learned and prepare you for moving ahead with the new subject.

In Spain women often greet with one or two kisses on the cheek and men shake other men's hands, although men may kiss or embrace younger male relatives or close friends. In more formal situations – among strangers or in a business context – a handshake is the norm.

¡Hola!
o-lah
Hello!

Words to remember (2 minutes)

Look at these greetings and say them aloud. Conceal the text on the left with the cover flap and try to remember the Spanish for each item. Check your answers.

Buenos días. *bwenos deeyas*	Good morning/day.
Me llamo Ana. *may yamoh anna*	My name is Ana.
Encantado/-a. *enkan-tadoh/-ah*	Pleased to meet you (man/woman speaking).
Buenas tardes (noches). *bwenas tardes (noches)*	Good afternoon/evening (night).

Cultural tip The Spanish frequently address people as **señor** (*sir*), **señora** (*madam*, for older women), and **señorita** (*miss*, for young women). With first names use **Don** for men or **Doña** for women: **Don Juan**, **Doña Ana**.

In conversation: formal (3 minutes)

Buenos días. Me llamo Concha García.
bwenos deeyas. may yamoh konchah garthee-ah

Good day. My name's Concha García.

Señor López, encantado.
senyor lopeth, enkan-tadoh

Mr López, pleased to meet you.

Encantada.
enkan-tadah

Pleased to meet you.

4 Put into practice (3 minutes)

Join in this conversation. Read the Spanish beside the pictures on the left and then follow the instructions to make your reply. Then test yourself by concealing the answers on the right with the cover flap.

Buenas tardes señor.
bwenas tardes senyor

Buenas tardes señora.
bwenas tardes senyorah

Good evening, sir.

Say: Good evening, madam.

Me llamo Julia.
may yamoh hoolya

Encantado.
enkan-tadoh

My name is Julia.

Say: Pleased to meet you.

5 Useful phrases (3 minutes)

Read these phrases aloud several times and try to memorize them. Conceal the Spanish with the cover flap and test yourself.

What's your name?	**¿Cómo se llama?** *komo seh yamah*
Goodbye.	**Adiós.** *addy-os*
Thank you.	**Gracias.** *grathyas*
See you soon/tomorrow.	**Hasta pronto/mañana.** *astah prontoh/manyanah*

6 In conversation: informal (3 minutes)

Entonces, ¿hasta mañana?
entonthes, astah manyanah

So, see you tomorrow?

Sí, adiós.
see, addy-os

Yes, goodbye.

Adiós. Hasta pronto.
addy-os. astah prontoh

Goodbye. See you soon.

1 Warm up (1 minute)

Say "hello" and "goodbye" in Spanish. (pp.8-9)

Now say "My name is...". (pp.8-9)

Say "sir" and "madam". (pp.8-9)

LAS RELACIONES
Relatives

The Spanish equivalents of *mum* and *dad* are **mamá** and **papá**. The male plural can refer to both sexes, for example - **niños** (*boys* and *children*), **padres** (*fathers* and *parents*), **abuelos** (*grandfathers* and *grandparents*), **tíos** (*uncles* and *aunt* and *uncle*), **hermanos** (*brothers* and *siblings*), and so on.

2 Match and repeat (5 minutes)

Look at the people in this scene and match their numbers with the list at the side. Read the Spanish words aloud. Now, conceal the list with the cover flap and test yourself.

❶ **la hermana**
   lah airmanah

❷ **el abuelo**
   el abweloh

❸ **el padre**
   el pahdray

❹ **el hermano**
   el airmanoh

❺ **la abuela**
   lah abwelah

❻ **la hija**
   lah ee-hah

❼ **la madre**
   lah mahdray

❽ **el hijo**
   el ee-hoh

grandfather ❷   ❸ father

sister ❶

❹ brother

❺ grandmother   ❻ daughter   ❼ mother   ❽ son

Conversational tip In Spanish, things as well as people are masculine or feminine - for example, *wine* is masculine (**el vino**) but *milk* is feminine (**la leche**). Use **los** and **las** for masculine and feminine plurals, respectively. For *a/an*, use **un** for masculine and **una** for feminine items.

3 Words to remember: relatives (4 minutes)

el marido
el mareedoh
husband

la mujer
lah moo-hair
wife

Estoy casado/-a.
estoy kasadoh/-ah
I'm married (m/f).

Familiarize yourself with these words. Read them aloud several times and try to memorize them. Conceal the Spanish with the cover flap and test yourself.

father/mother-in-law	**el suegro/la suegra** *el swegroh/lah swegrah*
stepfather	**el padrastro** *el padras-troh*
stepmother	**la madrastra** *lah madras-trah*
children (male/female)	**los niños/las niñas** *los neenyos/las neenyas*
uncle/aunt	**el tío/la tía** *el tee-oh/ lah tee-ah*
cousin	**el primo/la prima** *el preemoh/lah preemah*
I have four children.	**Tengo cuatro niños.** *tengoh kwatroh neenyos*
I have two stepdaughters and a stepson.	**Tengo dos hijastras y un hijastro.** *tengoh dos ee-hastras ee oon ee-hastroh*

4 Words to remember: numbers (3 minutes)

Memorize these words and then test yourself using the cover flap.

Careful when you use the number *one*. When you use **uno** in front of a word it changes to **un** or **una**, depending on whether that word is masculine or feminine. For example: **Tengo un hijo** *(I have one son)*, **Tengo una hija** *(I have one daughter)*.

one	**uno/-a**	*oonoh/-ah*
two	**dos**	*dos*
three	**tres**	*tres*
four	**cuatro**	*kwatroh*
five	**cinco**	*theenkoh*
six	**seis**	*seys*
seven	**siete**	*syetay*
eight	**ocho**	*ochoh*
nine	**nueve**	*nwebay*
ten	**diez**	*dyeth*

5 Say it (2 minute)

I have five sons.

I have three sisters and a brother.

I have two children.

1 Warm up (1 minute)

Say the Spanish for as many members of the family as you can. (pp.10-11)

Say "I have two sons". (pp.10-11)

MI FAMILIA
My family

There are two ways of saying *you* in Spanish, **usted** for formal situations and **tú** in informal ones. There is also a formal way of saying *your* – **su** (singular) and **sus** (plural): **usted y su mujer** (*you and your wife*), **¿Son ésos sus hijos?** (*Are those your sons?*). **Su** and **sus** also mean *his* and *her*.

2 Words to remember (5 minutes)

Say these words aloud a few times. Conceal the Spanish with the cover flap and try to remember the Spanish word for each item.

mi *mee*	my (with singular)
mis *mees*	my (with plural)
tu *too*	your (informal with singular)
tus *toos*	your (informal with plural)
su *soo*	your (formal with singular)
sus *soos*	your (formal with plural)
su *soo*	his/her (with singular) their (with singular)
sus *soos*	his/her (with plural) their (with plural)

Éstos son mis padres.
estos son mees pahdres
These are my parents.

3 In conversation (4 minutes)

¿Tiene usted niños?
tyenay oosted neenyos

Do you have any children?

Sí, tengo dos hijas.
see, tengoh dos ee-has

Yes, I have two daughters.

Éstas son mis hijas. ¿Y usted?
estas son mees ee-has. ee oosted

These are my daughters. And you?

Conversational tip The Spanish ask a question by simply raising the pitch of the voice at the end of a statement: **¿Quieres un poco de vino?** (*Do you want a little wine?*). Notice the upside-down question mark (¿) written at the beginning of the question. You will also see an upside-down exclamation mark, as in **¡Hola!** (*Hello!*).

4 Useful phrases (3 minutes)

Read these phrases aloud several times and try to memorize them. Conceal the Spanish with the cover flap and test yourself.

Do you have any brothers? (formal)	**¿Tiene usted hermanos?** *tyenay oosted airmanos*
Do you have any brothers? (informal)	**¿Tienes hermanos?** *tyenes airmanos*

This is my husband.	**Éste es mi marido.** *estay es mee mareedoh*
That's my wife.	**Ésa es mi mujer.** *esah es mee moo-hair*

Is that your sister? (formal)	**¿Es ésa su hermana?** *es esah soo airmanah*
Is that your sister? (informal)	**¿Es ésa tu hermana?** *es esah too airmanah*

5 Say it (2 minutes)

Do you have any brothers and sisters? (formal)

Do you have any children? (informal)

I have two sisters.

This is my wife, María.

No, pero tengo un hijastro.
noh, peroh tengoh oon ee-hastroh

No, but I have a stepson.

1 Warm up (1 minute)

Say "See you soon".
(pp.8-9)

Say "I am married"
(pp.10-11) and "I have
a wife". (pp.12-13)

SER Y TENER
To be and to have

Two of the most important verbs are **ser** (to be)
and **tener** (to have). Note that there are different
ways of saying you, we, and they, with formal and
informal, singular and plural, and masculine
and feminine forms. Pronouns (I, you, etc.) are
omitted where the sense is clear.

2 Ser: to be (5 minutes)

Familiarize yourself with ser (to be). When you are
confident, practise the sample sentences below.
Note: there is another verb meaning "to be" -
estar, which is discussed on page 49.

yo soy *yoh soy*	I am
tú eres *too eh-res*	you are (informal singular)
usted es *oosted es*	you are (formal singular)
él/ella es *el/eh-yah es*	he/she is
nosotros/-as somos *nosotros/-as somos*	we are (masculine/ feminine)
vosotros/-as sois *bosotros/-as soys*	you are (informal plural, m/f)
ustedes son *oostedes son*	you are (formal plural)
ellos/-as son *eh-yos/-yas son*	they are (masculine/ feminine)

Yo soy inglesa.
yoh soy eenglesah
I'm English.

¿De dónde es usted? *day donday es oosted*	Where are you from?
Es mi hermana. *es mee airmanah*	She is my sister.
Somos españoles. *somos espanyoles*	We're Spanish.

3 Tener: to have (5 minutes)

Practise **tener** (to have) and the sample sentences, then test yourself.

I have	**yo tengo** *yoh tengoh*
you have (informal singular)	**tú tienes** *too tyenes*
you have (formal singular)	**usted tiene** *oosted tyenay*
he/she has	**él/ella tiene** *el/eh-yah tyenay*
we have (masculine/feminine)	**nosotros/-as tenemos** *nosotros/-as tenaymos*
you have (informal plural, m/f)	**vosotros/-as teneis** *bosotros/-as tenays*
you have (formal plural)	**ustedes tienen** *oostedes tyenen*
they have (masculine/feminine)	**ellos/-as tienen** *eh-yos/-yas tyenen*

¿Tiene rosas rojas?
tyenay rosas rohas
Do you have red roses?

He has a meeting.	**Tiene una reunión.** *tyenay oonah re-oonyon*
Do you have a mobile phone?	**¿Tiene usted móvil?** *tyenay oosted mobeel?*
How many brothers and sisters do you have?	**¿Cuántos hermanos tiene usted?** *kwantos airmanos tyenay oosted*

4 Negatives (4 minutes)

la bicicleta
lah beetheekletah
bicycle

No tengo coche.
noh tengoh kochay
I don't have a car.

It is easy to make sentences negative in Spanish, just put **no** in front of the verb: **No somos americanos** (We're not American).

I'm not Spanish.	**No soy español.** *noh soy espanyol*
He's not a vegetarian.	**No es vegetariano.** *noh es be-hetaryanoh*
We don't have any children.	**No tenemos niños.** *noh tenaymos neenyos*

Respuestas
Answers (Cover with flap)

REPASE Y REPITA
Review and repeat

1 How many

❶ **tres**
tres

❷ **nueve**
nwebay

❸ **cuatro**
kwatroh

❹ **dos**
dos

❺ **ocho**
ochoh

❻ **diez**
dyeth

❼ **cinco**
theenkoh

❽ **siete**
syetay

❾ **seis**
seys

1 How many (2 minutes)

Cover the answers with the flap. Then say these Spanish numbers out loud. Check you have remembered the Spanish correctly.

3 ❶ 9 ❷ 4 ❸
2 ❹ 8 ❺ 10 ❻
5 7 ❼ 6 ❾
❽

2 Hello

❶ **Buenos días. Me llamo... [your name].**
bwenos deeyas. may yamoh...

❷ **Encantado/-a.**
enkan-tadoh/-ah

❸ **Sí, y tengo dos hijos. ¿Y usted?**
see, ee tengoh dos ee-hos. ee oosted

❹ **Adiós. Hasta mañana.**
addy-os. astah manyanah

2 Hello (4 minutes)

You are talking to someone you have just met. Join in the conversation, replying in Spanish following the English prompts.

Buenos días. Me llamo María.
❶ Answer the greeting and give your name.

Éste es mi marido, Juan.
❷ Say "Pleased to meet you".

¿Está usted casado/-a?
❸ Say "Yes, and I have two sons. And you?"

Nosotros tenemos tres hijos.
❹ Say "Goodbye. See you tomorrow".

3 To have or be (5 minutes)

Fill in the blanks with the correct form of **tener**
(*to have*) or **ser** (*to be*). Check you have remembered
the Spanish correctly.

❶ Yo _____ inglesa.

❷ Nosotros _____ cuatro niños.

❸ Yo no _____ feliz.

❹ ¿ _____ tú coche?

❺ Él _____ mi marido.

❻ Yo no _____ teléfono móvil.

❼ Tú no _____ español.

❽ ¿ _____ usted hijos?

3 To have or be

❶ **soy**
soy

❷ **tenemos**
tenaymos

❸ **soy**
soy

❹ **tienes**
tyenes

❺ **es**
es

❻ **tengo**
tengoh

❼ **eres**
eh-res

❽ **tiene**
tyenay

4 Family (4 minutes)

Say the Spanish for each of the numbered family
members. Check you have remembered the
Spanish correctly.

grandfather ❷ ❸ father

sister ❶ ❹ brother

❺ grandmother ❻ daughter ❼ mother ❽ son

4 Family

❶ **la hermana**
lah airmanah

❷ **el abuelo**
el abweloh

❸ **el padre**
el pahdray

❹ **el hermano**
el airmanoh

❺ **la abuela**
lah abwelah

❻ **la hija**
lah ee-ha

❼ **la madre**
lah mahdray

❽ **el hijo**
el ee-hoh

EN LA CAFETERÍA
In the café

1 Warm up (1 minute)

Count to ten. (pp.10-11)

Remind yourself how to say "hello" and "goodbye". (pp.8-9)

Ask "Do you have a son?" (pp.14-15)

In a Spanish café you can get bread and pastries with your coffee in the mornings. **Churros** (fried dough sticks) are a typical Spanish snack. You can either sit at the counter or have waiter service at a table. It is usual to tip the waiter, but a few coins is usually enough.

el chocolate
el chokolatay
chocolate

2 Words to remember (5 minutes)

Familiarize yourself with these words.

el té con limón *el tay kon leemon*	tea with lemon
el café descafeinado *el kafay deskafeynadoh*	decaffeinated coffee
el cortado *el kortadoh*	espresso with a bit of milk
la mermelada *lah mermeladah*	jam
la tostada con mantequilla *lah tostadah kon mantekee-yah*	toast with butter

el café solo
el kafay soloh
espresso

Cultural tip A standard coffee is small and black; if you want it any other way, you'll need to specify. If you want tea with milk, ask for **té con leche**. If you just ask for **té**, you are likely to get tea with lemon.

3 In conversation (4 minutes)

Buenos días. Me pone un café con leche.
bwenos deeyas. may ponay oon kafay kon lechay

Hello. I'll have a white coffee, please.

¿Eso es todo?
esoh es todoh

Is that all?

¿Tiene churros?
tyenay choorros

Do you have any churros?

4 Useful phrases (5 minutes)

Learn these phrases. Read the English under the pictures and say the phrase in Spanish as shown on the right. Then cover the Spanish with the cover flap and test yourself.

los churros
los choorros
churros

el azúcar
el ah-thookar
sugar

Me pone un café.
may ponay oon kafay

I'll have a black coffee.

¿Eso es todo?
esoh es todoh

Is that all?

Yo voy a tomar churros.
yoh boy ah tomar choorros

I'm going to have some churros.

¿Cuánto es?
kwantoh es

How much is that?

el café con leche
el kafay kon lechay
white coffee

Sí, señor.
see, senyor

Yes, sir.

Gracias. ¿Cuánto es?
grathyas. kwantoh es

Thank you. How much is that?

Cuatro euros, por favor.
kwatroh eh-ooros, por fabor

Four euros, please.

EN EL RESTAURANTE
In the restaurant

Warm up (1 minute)

Ask "How much is that?" (pp.18-19)

Say "I don't have a brother". (pp.14-15)

Ask "Do you have any churros?" (pp.18-19)

There are a variety of different types of eating places in Spain. In a bar or **tasca** you can find a few **tapas** or snacks. Lunch is the main meal of the day, but if you are not very hungry, many restaurants offer **tapas** at the bar, which is usually very good value for a light meal.

Words to remember (3 minutes)

Memorize these words. Conceal the Spanish with the cover flap and test yourself.

la carta *lah kartah*	menu
la carta de vinos *lah kartah day beenos*	wine list
los entrantes *los entrantes*	starters
el plato principal *el platoh preentheepal*	main course
los postres *los postres*	desserts
el desayuno *el desah-yoonoh*	breakfast
el almuerzo *el almooairthoh*	lunch
la cena *lah thenah*	dinner

cup **8**

saucer **7**

6 spoon

4 knife

fork **5**

In conversation (4 minutes)

Hola. Una mesa para cuatro, por favor.
o-lah. oonah mesah parah kwatroh, por fabor

Hello. A table for four, please.

¿Tiene una reserva?
tyenay oonah reserbah

Do you have a reservation?

Sí, a nombre de Cortés.
see, ah nombray day kortes

Yes, in the name of Cortés.

4 Match and repeat (4 minutes)

Look at the numbered objects on this table and match them with the items in the vocabulary list at the side. Read the Spanish words aloud. Now, conceal the list with the cover flap and test yourself.

glass ❶

❷ napkin

plate ❸

❶ **la copa**
lah kopah

❷ **la servilleta**
lah serbee-yetah

❸ **el plato**
el platoh

❹ **el cuchillo**
el koochee-yoh

❺ **el tenedor**
el tenedor

❻ **la cuchara**
lah koocharah

❼ **el platillo**
el plateeyoh

❽ **la taza**
lah tathah

5 Useful phrases (4 minutes)

Learn these phrases and then test yourself using the cover flap to conceal the Spanish.

What do you have for dessert?	**¿Qué tiene de postre?** *kay tyenay day postray*
The bill, please.	**La cuenta, por favor.** *lah kwentah, por fabor*

Muy bien. ¿Qué mesa le gustaría?
mwee byen. kay mesah le goostareeyah

Very good. Which table would you like?

Cerca de la ventana, por favor.
therkah day lah bentanah, por fabor

Near the window please.

Síganme, por favor.
seegan-may, por fabor.

Follow me, please.

1 Warm up (1 minute)

What are "breakfast", "lunch", and "dinner" in Spanish? (pp.20-1)

Say "I", "you" (informal), "he", "she", "we", "you" (plural/formal), "they" (masculine), "they" (feminine). (pp.14-15)

QUERER
To want

Querer (*to want*) is a verb that is essential to everyday conversation. There is also a polite form, **quisiera** (*I'd like*). Use this when requesting something because quiero (*I want*) may sound too strong: **¿Qué quiere beber?** (*What do you want to drink?*); **Quisiera una cerveza** (*I'd like a beer*).

2 Querer: to want (6 minutes)

Say the different forms of **querer** (*to want*) aloud. Use the cover flap to test yourself and, when you are confident, practise the sample sentences below.

yo quiero *yoh kyairoh*	I want
tú quieres/usted quiere *too kyaires/oosted kyairay*	you want (singular, informal/formal)
él/ella quiere *el/eh-yah kyairay*	he/she wants
nosotros/-as queremos *nosotros/-as keraymos*	we want (masculine/feminine)
vosotros/-as queréis/ ustedes quieren *bosotros/-as kerays/ oostedes kyairen*	you want (plural, informal/formal)
ellos/-as quieren *eh-yos/-as-yas kyairen*	they want (masculine/feminine)
¿Quieres vino? *kyaires beenoh?*	Do you want some wine?
Quiere un coche nuevo. *kyairay oon kochay nweboh*	She wants a new car.

Quiero caramelos.
kyairoh karamelos
I want some sweets.

Conversational tip Although it may sound rude to you, Spaniards don't say *please* (**por favor**) or *thank you* (**gracias**) very often, and they hardly ever say *excuse me* (**perdón**) or *I'm sorry* (**lo siento**), but they use the tone of their voices and choice of words to imply politeness, such as **quisiera** (*I'd like*) instead of **quiero** (*I want*).

3 Polite requests (4 minutes)

Practise the following sample phrases that use
quisiera (*I'd like*), the form of **quiero** (*I want*)
that is used for polite requests.

I'd like a beer. **Quisiera un cerveza.**
keesyairah oon
therbaythah

I'd like a table for tonight. **Quisiera una mesa para
esta noche.**
keesyairah oonah mesah
parah estah nocheh

I'd like to see the
menu, please. **Quisiera ver la carta,
por favor.**
keesyairah ber lah kartah,
por fabor

4 Put into practice (4 minutes)

Join in this conversation. Read the Spanish beside
the pictures on the left and follow the instructions
to make your reply. Then test yourself by concealing
the answers using the cover flap.

**Buenas tardes señor.
¿Tiene una reserva?**
bwenas tardes senyor.
tyeneh oonah reserbah

**No, pero quisiera
una mesa para tres.**
noh, peroh keesyairah
oonah mesah parah tres

Good evening, sir. Do you
have a reservation?

Say: No, but I would like a
table for three.

**Muy bien. ¿Qué mesa
le gustaría?**
mwee byen. kay mesah
le goostareeyah

**Cerca de la ventana,
por favor.**
therkah day lah bentanah,
por fabor

Very good. Which table
would you like?

Say: Near the
window please.

LOS PLATOS
Dishes

1 Warm up (1 minute)

Say "She's happy" and "I'm not sure". (pp.14-15)

Ask "Do you have churros?" (pp.18-19)

Say "I'd like a white coffee". (pp.18-19)

Spain offers a large variety of regional dishes. Plenty of garlic and olive oil are a feature of many typical dishes. Not many restaurants offer a vegetarian menu, but there are, however, many traditional Spanish dishes that do not contain meat. Ask your waiter for advice.

Cultural tip At lunch time, you will find that many restaurants offer **el menú del día** (*the day's set menu*). This is usually a three-course meal, with bread and drink included in the price.

2 Match and repeat (4 minutes)

Match the numbered items to the Spanish words in the panel.

1 las verduras
las berdooras

2 la fruta
lah frootah

3 el queso
el kesoh

4 los frutos secos
los frootos sekos

5 la sopa
lah sopah

6 las aves
las ahbes

7 el pescado
el peskadoh

8 la pasta
lah pastah

9 el marisco
el mareeskoh

10 la carne
lah karnay

vegetables **1**

fruit **2**

cheese **3**

5 soup

poultry **6**

8 pasta

9 seafood

3 Words to remember: cooking methods (3 minutes)

The ending often varies depending on the gender of item described.

fried (m/f)	**frito/-a** *freetoh/-ah*
grilled	**a la plancha** *ah lah planchah*
roasted (m/f)	**asado/-a** *ahsadoh/-ah*
boiled (m/f)	**hervido/-a** *erbeedoh/-ah*
steamed	**al vapor** *al bapor*
rare (m/f)	**poco hecho/-a** *pokoh eh-choh/-ah*

Quisiera mi filete bien hecho.
keesyairah mee feeletay byen eh-choh
I'd like my steak well done.

6 Say it (2 minutes)

What is **tortilla**?

I'm allergic to seafood.

I'd like a beer.

nuts 4

4 Words to remember: drinks (3 minutes)

Familiarize yourself with these words.

water	**el agua** *el ahgwah*
fizzy water	**el agua con gas** *el ahgwah kon gas*
still water	**el agua sin gas** *el ahgwah seen gas*
wine	**el vino** *el beenoh*
beer	**la cerveza** *lah thairbaythah*
fruit juice	**el zumo** *el thoomoh*

fish 7

10 meat

5 Useful phrases (2 minutes)

Learn these phrases and then test yourself.

I am a vegetarian. (m/f)	**Soy vegetariano/-a.** *soy be-hetareeanoh/-ah*
I am allergic to nuts. (m/f)	**Soy alérgico/-a a los frutos secos.** *soy ahler-heekoh/-ah ah los frootos sekos*
What is "conejo"?	**¿Qué es "conejo"?** *kay es kone-hoh*

REPASE Y REPITA
Review and repeat

Respuestas
Answers (Cover with flap)

1 What food?

1 los frutos secos
los frootos sekos

2 el marisco
el mareeskoh

3 la carne
lah karnay

4 el azúcar
el ah-thookar

5 la copa
lah kopah

1 What food? (4 minutes)

Name the numbered items.

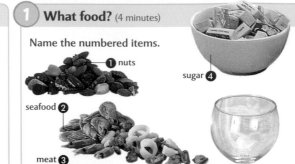

1 nuts
sugar **4**
seafood **2**
meat **3**
glass **5**

2 This is my...

1 Ésta es mi mujer.
estah es mee moo-hair

2 Aquí están sus hijas.
ahkee estan soos ee-has

3 Su mesa es de no fumadores.
soo mesah es day noh foomadores

2 This is my... (4 minutes)

Say these phrases in Spanish. Use **mi**(-**s**), **tu**(-**us**) or **su**(-**s**).

1 This is my wife.
2 Here are her daughters.
3 Their table is non-smoking.

3 I'd like...

1 Quisiera un café.
keesyairah oon kafay

2 Quisiera churros.
keesyairah choorros

3 Quisiera azúcar.
keesyairah ah-thookar

4 Quisiera un café con leche.
keesyairah oon kafay kon lechay

3 I'd like... (3 minutes)

Say "I'd like" the following:

1 black coffee   churros **2**   **3** sugar

white coffee **4**

6 pasta
knife 7
8 cheese
beer 10
9 napkin

1 What food?

6 la pasta
lah pastah

7 el cuchillo
el koochee-yoh

8 el queso
el kesoh

9 la servilleta
lah serbee-yetah

10 la cerveza
lah thairbaythah

4 Restaurant (4 minutes)

You arrive at a restaurant. Join in the conversation, replying in Spanish following the English prompts.

Buenas tardes señora, señor.
1 Ask for a table for six.

¿Fumadores o no fumadores?
2 Say: non-smoking.

Síganme, por favor.
3 Ask for the menu.

¿Quiere la carta de vinos?
4 Say: No. Fizzy water, please.

Muy bien.
5 Say you don't have a glass.

4 Restaurant

1 **Buenas tardes, quisiera una mesa para seis.**
bwenas tardes, keesyairah oonah mesah parah seys

2 **No fumadores.**
noh foomadores

3 **La carta, por favor.**
lah kartah, por fabor

4 **No. Agua con gas, por favor.**
noh. ahgwah kon gas, por fabor

5 **No tengo copa.**
noh tengoh kopah

LOS DÍAS Y LOS MESES
Days and months

Say "he is" and "they are". (pp.14–15)

Say "he is not" and "they are not". (pp.14–15)

What is Spanish for "the children"? (pp.10–11)

In Spanish, *days of the week* (**los días de la semana**) and *months* (**los meses**) do not have capital letters Notice that you use **en** with months: **en abril** (*in April*), but **el** or **los** with days: **el/los lunes** (*on Monday/Mondays*).

2 Words to remember: days of the week (5 minutes)

Familiarize yourself with these words and test yourself using the cover flap.

lunes *loones*	Monday
martes *martes*	Tuesday
miércoles *myairkoles*	Wednesday
jueves *hwebes*	Thursday
viernes *byernes*	Friday
sábado *sabadoh*	Saturday
domingo *domeengoh*	Sunday
hoy *oy*	today
mañana *manyanah*	tomorrow
ayer *ah-yair*	yesterday

Nos reunimos mañana.
mos reh-ooneemos manyanah
We meet tomorrow.

Tengo una reserva para hoy.
tengoh oonah reserbah parah oy
I have a reservation for today.

3 Useful phrases: days (2 minutes)

Learn these phrases and then test yourself using the cover flap.

La reunión no es el martes. *lah reh-oonyon noh es el martes*	The meeting isn't on Tuesday.
Trabajo los domingos. *traba-hoh los domeengos*	I work on Sundays.

4 Words to remember: months (5 minutes)

Familiarize yourself with these words and test yourself using the cover flap.

Nuestro aniversario es en julio.
nwestroh aneebairsaree-oh es en hoolee-oh
Our anniversary is in July.

Navidad es en diciembre.
nabeedad es en deethyembray
Christmas is in December.

January	**enero**	*ehneroh*
February	**febrero**	*febreroh*
March	**marzo**	*marthoh*
April	**abril**	*abreel*
May	**mayo**	*mah-yoh*
June	**junio**	*hoonee-oh*
July	**julio**	*hoolee-oh*
August	**agosto**	*agostoh*
September	**septiembre**	*septyembray*
October	**octubre**	*oktoobray*
November	**noviembre**	*nobyembray*
December	**diciembre**	*deethyembray*
month	**el mes**	*el mes*
year	**el año**	*el anyoh*

5 Useful phrases: months (2 minutes)

Learn these phrases and then test yourself using the cover flap.

My children are on holiday in August.
Mis hijos están de vacaciones en agosto.
mees ee-hos estan day bakathyones en agostoh

My birthday is in June.
Mi cumpleaños es en junio.
mee koomplay-anyos es en hoonee-oh

LA HORA Y LOS NÚMEROS
Time and numbers

1 **Warm up** (1 minute)

Count in Spanish from
1 to 10. (pp.10-11)

Say "I have a reservation".
(pp.20-1)

Say "The meeting is on
Wednesday". (pp.28-9)

The hour is preceded by **la** as in **la una** (*one o'clock*)
and **las** for the other numbers: **las dos**, **las tres**, and
so on. In English the minutes come first: ten to five,
in Spanish the hour comes first: **las cinco menos
diez** (*five minus ten*).

2 **Words to remember: time** (4 minutes)

Memorize how to tell the time in Spanish.

la una *lah oonah*	one o'clock
la una y cinco *lah oonah ee theenkoh*	five past one
la una y cuarto *lah oonah ee kwartoh*	quarter past one
la una y veinte *lah oonah ee beyntay*	twenty past one
la una y media *lah oonah ee medee-ah*	half past one
las dos menos cuarto *las dos menos kwartoh*	quarter to two
las dos menos diez *las dos menos dyeth*	ten to two

3 **Useful phrases** (2 minutes)

Learn these phrases and then test yourself
using the cover flap.

¿Qué hora es? *kay orah es*	What time is it?
¿A qué hora quiere el desayuno? *ah kay orah kyairay el desah-yoonoh*	What time do you want breakfast?
La reunión es a mediodía. *lah reh-oonyon es ah maydyodee-ah*	The meeting is at midday.

4 Words to remember: higher numbers (6 minutes)

To say 21 you use **veinti** and add **uno** (*one*): **veintiuno**. Successive numbers are created in the same way – for example, **veintidós** (22), **veintitrés** (23), and so on. After 30 link the numbers with **y** (*and*): **treinta y uno** (31), **cuarenta y cinco** (45), **sesenta y seis** (66).

Note the special forms used for 500, 700, and 900: **quinientos**, **setecientos**, and **novecientos**.

Quiero el autobús cincuenta y tres.
kyairoh el aootoboos theenkwentah ee tres
I want the number 53 bus.

eleven	**once**	*onthay*
twelve	**doce**	*dothay*
thirteen	**trece**	*trethay*
fourteen	**catorce**	*katorthay*
fifteen	**quince**	*keenthay*
sixteen	**dieciséis**	*deeaytheeseyees*
seventeen	**diecisiete**	*deeaytheesyeytay*
eighteen	**dieciocho**	*deeaythyochoh*
nineteen	**diecinueve**	*deeaythynwebay*
twenty	**veinte**	*beyntay*
thirty	**treinta**	*treyntah*
forty	**cuarenta**	*kwarentah*
fifty	**cincuenta**	*theenkwentah*
sixty	**sesenta**	*sesentah*
seventy	**setenta**	*setentah*
eighty	**ochenta**	*ochentah*
ninety	**noventa**	*nobentah*
hundred	**cien**	*theeayn*
two hundred	**doscientos**	*dos-theeayntos*
five hundred	**quinientos**	*keeneeayntos*
thousand	**mil**	*meel*
two thousand	**dos mil**	*dos meel*
one million	**un millón**	*oon mee-yon*

5 Say it (2 minutes)

25

68

84

91

five to ten

half past eleven

What time is lunch?

LAS CITAS
Appointments

Say the days of the week. (pp.28-9)

Say "three o'clock". (pp.30-1)

What's the Spanish for "today", "tomorrow", and "yesterday"? (pp.28-9)

Business in Spain is generally conducted more formally than in Britain or the United States. The Spanish also tend to leave the office for the lunch hour, often having a sit-down meal. Remember to use the formal forms of *you* (**usted**, **ustedes**) in business situations.

Bienvenido.
byenveneedoh
Welcome.

2   Useful phrases (5 minutes)

Learn these phrases and then test yourself.

¿Nos reunimos mañana? *nos reh-ooneemos manyanah*	Shall we meet tomorrow?
¿Con quién? *kon kee-en*	With whom?
¿Cuándo está libre? *kwandoh esta leebray*	When are you free?
Lo siento, estoy ocupado(-a). *loh syentoh, estoy okoopadoh(-ah)*	I'm sorry, I am busy.
¿Qué tal el jueves? *keh tal el hwebes*	How about Thursday?
A mí me va bien. *ah mee may bah byen*	That's good for me.

el apretón de manos
el apreton day manos
handshake

3   In conversation (4 minutes)

Buenos días. Tengo una cita.
bwenos deeyas. tengoh oonah theetah

Good morning. I have an appointment.

¿Con quién es la cita?
kon kee-en es lah theetah

With whom is the appointment?

Con el Señor Montoya.
kon el senyor montoyah

With Mr Montoya.

4 **Put into practice** (5 minutes)

Join in this conversation. Read the Spanish beside the pictures on the left and then follow the instructions to make your reply. Then test yourself by concealing the answers on the right with the cover flap.

¿Nos reunimos el jueves?
nos reh-ooneemos el hwebes?

Shall we meet Thursday?

Say: Sorry, I'm busy.

Lo siento, estoy ocupado(-a).
loh syentoh, estoy okoopadoh(-ah)

¿Cuándo está libre?
kwandoh esta leebray

When are you free?

Say: Tuesday afternoon.

El martes por la tarde.
el martes por lah tarday

A mí me va bien.
ah mee may bah byen

That's good for me.

Ask: At what time?

¿A qué hora?
ah kay orah

A las cuatro, si a usted le va bien.
ah las kwatroh, see ah oosted le bah byen

At four o'clock, if that's good for you.

Say: Yes, it's good for me.

Sí, me va bien.
see, may bah byen

Muy bien. ¿A qué hora?
mwee byen. ah kay orah?

Very good. What time?

A las tres, pero llego un poco tarde.
ah las tres, peroh yegoh oon pokoh tarday

At three o'clock, but I'm a little late.

No se preocupe. Tome asiento, por favor.
noh say pre-ohkoopay. tomay asyaintoh, por fabor

Don't worry. Take a seat, please.

POR TELÉFONO
On the telephone

Say "I'm sorry". (pp.32-3)

What is the Spanish for "I'd like an appointment". (pp.32-3)

How do you say "when?" in Spanish? (pp.32-3)

The emergency number for police, ambulance, or fire services is 112. For directory enquiries dial 11818. If you are planning to make a lot of phone calls from Spain, the most cost-effective option is to buy a Spanish SIM card for your mobile phone, or even a cheap mobile phone with a top-up SIM.

2 **Match and repeat** (4 minutes)

Match the numbered items to the Spanish in the panel on the left, then test yourself.

1 el cargador
el kargador

2 el teléfono
el telefonoh

3 el contestador
automático
*el kontestador
aootomateekoh*

4 los auriculares
los aooreekoolares

5 el móvil
el mobeel

6 la tarjeta SIM
lah tarhetah seem

charger **1**

telephone **2**

headphones **4**

5 mobile

3 **In conversation** (4 minutes)

Dígame, Susana Castillo al habla.
deegamay, soosanah kasteeyoh al ablah

Hello. Susana Castillo speaking.

Buenos días. Quisiera hablar con Julián López, por favor.
bwenos deeyas. keesyair-ah ablar kon hooleean lopeth, por fabor

Hello. I'd like to speak to Julián López, please.

¿De parte de quién?
day partay day kee-en?

Who's speaking?

SIM card **6**

Quisiera comprar una tarjeta SIM.
keesyairah komprar oonah tarhetah seem
I'd like to buy a SIM card.

3 answering machine

4 Useful phrases (4 minutes)

Practise these phrases and then test yourself using the cover flap.

I'd like the number for Juan.

Quisiera el número de Juan.
keesyairah el noomeroh dey hosay

I'd like to speak to María Alfaro.

Quisiera hablar con María Alfaro.
keesyairah ablar kon mareeah alfaroh

Can I leave a message?

¿Puedo dejar un mensaje?
pwedoh dehar oon mensahay

Sorry, I have the wrong number.

Perdone, me he equivocado de número.
perdonay, may ay ekeebokadoh day noomeroh

5 Say it (2 minutes)

I'd like to speak to Mr Girona.

Can I leave a message for Antonio?

José Ortega, de Imprentas Lacuesta.
hosay ortegah, day eemprentas lakwestah

José Ortega of Lacuesta Printers.

Lo siento. La línea está comunicando.
loh syaintoh. lah leeneah estah komooneekandoh

I'm sorry. The line is busy.

¿Le puede decir que me llame, por favor?
lay pweday detheer kay may yamay, por fabor

Can you ask him to call me, please?

REPASE Y REPITA
Review and repeat

Respuestas
Answers (Cover with flap)

1 Sums

❶ **dieciséis**
deeaythee<u>say</u>ees

❷ **treinta y nueve**
<u>treyn</u>tah ee <u>nwe</u>bay

❸ **cincuenta y tres**
theen<u>kwen</u>tah ee tres

❹ **setenta y cuatro**
se<u>ten</u>tah ee <u>kwa</u>troh

❺ **noventa y nueve**
no<u>ben</u>tah ee <u>nwe</u>bay

1 Sums (4 minutes)

Say the answers
to these sums out
loud in Spanish.
Then check you have
remembered correctly.

❶ 10 + 6 = ?
❷ 14 + 25 = ?
❸ 66 - 13 = ?
❹ 40 + 34 = ?
❺ 90 + 9 = ?

3 Telephones (3 minutes)

What are the numbered
items in Spanish?

mobile ❶

❷ SIM card

2 I want...

❶ **Quiere**
<u>kyai</u>ray

❷ **quiere**
<u>kyai</u>ray

❸ **queremos**
ke<u>ray</u>mos

❹ **quieres**
<u>kyai</u>res

❺ **quieren**
<u>kyai</u>ren

❻ **quiero**
<u>kyai</u>roh

2 I want... (3 minutes)

Fill the gaps with the
correct form of
(*to want*).

❶ ¿ _____ usted un café?
❷ Ella _____ ir de vacaciones.
❸ Nosotros _____ una mesa para tres.
❹ Tú _____ una cerveza.
❺ Ellos _____ una mesa para dos.
❻ Yo _____ caramelos.

telephone ❸

answering ❹
machine

❺ headphones

Respuestas
Answers (Cover with flap)

3 Telephones

❶ **el móvil**
el mobeel

❷ **la tarjeta SIM**
lah tarhetah seem

❸ **el teléfono**
el telefonoh

❹ **el contestador automático**
el kontestador aootomateekoh

❺ **los auriculares**
los aooreekoolares

4 When? (2 minutes)

What do these sentences mean?

❶ Tengo una cita el lunes veinte de mayo.

❷ Mi cumpleaños es en septiembre.

❸ Hoy es domingo.

❹ No trabajo en agosto.

4 When?

❶ I have a meeting on Monday, 20th May.
❷ My birthday is in September.
❸ Today is Sunday.
❹ I don't work in August.

5 Time (3 minutes)

Say these times in Spanish.

❶ ❷ ❸ ❹ ❺ ❻

5 Time

❶ **la una**
lah oonah

❷ **la una y cinco**
la oonah ee theenkoh

❸ **la una y veinte**
lah oonah ee beyntay

❹ **la una y media**
lah oonah ee medee-ah

❺ **la una y cuarto**
lah oonah ee kwartoh

❻ **las dos menos diez**
las dos menos dyeth

1 Warm up (1 minute)

Count to 100 in tens.
(pp.10-11, pp.30-1)

Ask "What time is it?"
(pp.30-1)

Say "Half-past one".
(pp.30-1)

EN LA OFICINA DE BILLETES
At the ticket office

In Spain, commuter trains are very good value, clean, and efficient. Long-distance trains still offer smoking and non-smoking carriages, and the prices vary depending on what day you travel, blue days being the cheapest.

2 Words to remember (3 minutes)

Learn these words and then test yourself.

la estación *lah estathyon*	(train) station
la terminal *lah termeenal*	(bus) station
el billete *el beeyetay*	ticket
de ida *day eedah*	single
de ida y vuelta *day eedah ee bweltah*	return
de primera *day preemerah*	first class
de segunda *day segoondah*	second class
el descuento *el deskwentoh*	discount

el pasajero
el pasahairoh
passenger

la señal
lah senyal
sign

La estación está llena de gente.
lah estathyon estah yenah day hentay
The station is crowded.

3 In conversation (4 minutes)

Dos billetes para Bilbao, por favor.
dos beeyetes parah beeba-oh, por fabor

Two tickets for Bilbao, please.

¿De ida y vuelta?
day eedah y bweltah

Return?

Si.¿Necesito reservar asiento?
see. netheseetoh rreseerbar asyaintoh

Yes. Do I need to reserve seats?

4 Useful phrases (5 minutes)

Learn these phrases and then test yourself using the cover flap.

Mi tren va con retraso.
mee tren bah kon rretrasoh
My train is late.

el tren	el andén
el tren	*el anden*
train	platform

How much is a ticket to Madrid?	**¿Cuánto cuesta un billete para Madrid?** *kwantoh kwaystah oon beeyetay parah madreed*
Can I pay by credit card?	**¿Puedo pagar con tarjeta de crédito?** *pwedoh pagar kon tarhetah day kredeetoh*
Do I have to change?	**¿Tengo que cambiar?** *tengoh kay kambee-ar*
Which platform does the train leave from?	**¿De qué andén sale el tren?** *day kay anden salay el tren*
Are there any discounts?	**¿Hay algún descuento?** *ah-ee algoon deskwentoh*
What time does the train for Gijón leave?	**¿A qué hora sale el tren para Gijón?** *ah kay orah salay el tren parah geehon*

5 Say it (2 minutes)

Which platform does the train for Madrid leave from?

Three return tickets to Murcia, please.

Cultural tip Most train stations have automatic ticket machines that also take credit cards.

No hace falta. Cuarenta euros, por favor.
noh ahthay faltah. kwarentah eh-ooros, por fabor

That's not necessary. Forty euros, please.

¿Aceptan tarjetas de crédito?
ahtheptan tarhetas day kredeetoh

Do you accept credit cards?

Si. El tren sale del andén cinco.
see. el tren salay del anden theenkoh

Yes. The train leaves from platform five.

① Warm up (1 minute)

What is "train" in Spanish? (pp.38-9)

What does "¿De qué andén sale el tren?" mean? (pp.38-9)

Ask "When are you free?" (pp.32-3)

IR Y COGER
To go and to take

The verbs **ir** (*to go*) and **coger** (*to take*) allow you to create many useful sentences. Note that **coger** can also mean to catch: **coger una pelota** (*to catch a ball*), **coger un resfriado** (*to catch a cold*); to grab: **coger a alguien** (*to grab someone*); and to hold: **coger a un bebé** (*to hold a baby*).

② Ir: to go (6 minutes)

Spanish uses the same form of **ir** for both *I go* and *I am going*: **voy a Madrid** (*I am going to Madrid/I go to Madrid*). The same is true of other verbs - for example, **cojo el metro** (*I am taking the metro/I take the metro*).

yo voy *yoh boy*	I go
tú vas/usted va *too bas/oosted bah*	you go (informal/formal singular)
él/ella va *el/eh-yah bah*	he/she goes
nosotros(-as) vamos *nosotros(-as) bamos*	we go
vosotros(-as) vais/ ustedes van *bosotros(-as) baees/ oostedes ban*	you go (informal/formal plural)
ellos/ellas van *eh-yos/eh-yas ban*	they go

¿A dónde vas? *ah donday bas*	Where are you going?
Voy a Madrid. *boy ah madreed*	I am going to Madrid.

Voy a la Plaza de España.
boy ah lah plathah day espanyah
I am going to the Plaza de España.

Conversational tip You may have noticed that **de** (*of*) combines with **el** to produce **del** as in **Museo del Prado** (meaning literally *museum of the Prado*); **el menú del día** (*menu of the day*). In the same way, **a** (*to*) combines with **el** to produce **al**: **Voy al museo** (*I'm going to the museum*). With feminine and plural words **de** remains separate from **la**, **los**, and **las**.

3 Coger: to take (6 minutes)

Say the present tense of **coger** (to take) aloud. Use the cover flap to test yourself. When you are confident, practise the sentences below.

yo cojo *yoh kohoh*	I take
tú coges/usted coge *too kohes/oosted kohay*	you take (informal/ formal singular)
él/ella coge *el/eh-yah kohay*	he/she takes
nosotros(-as) cogemos *nosotros(-as) kohaymos*	we take
vosotros(-as) cogéis/ ustedes cogen *bosotros(-as) kohe-ees/ oostedes kohen*	you take (informal/ formal plural)
ellos/ellas cogen *eh-yos/eh-yas kohen*	they take

Yo cojo el metro todos los días.
yoh kohoh el metroh todos los deeyas
I take the metro every day.

No quiero coger un taxi. *noh kyairoh koher oon taksee*	I don't want to take a taxi.
Coja la primera a la izquierda. *kohah lah preemerah ah lah eethkyairdah*	Take the first on the left.

4 Put into practice (2 minutes)

Cover the text on the right and complete the dialogue in Spanish.

¿A dónde va? *ah donday bah*	**Voy a la Puerta del Sol.** *boy ah lah pwertah del sol*
Where are you going?	
Say: I'm going to the Puerta del Sol.	
¿Quiere coger el autobús? *kyairay koher el aootoboos*	**No, quiero ir en metro.** *noh, kyairoh eer en metroh*
Do you want to take the bus?	
Say: No, I want to go by metro.	

1 Warm up (1 minute)

Say "I don't want to take a taxi". (pp.40-41)

Ask "Where are you going?" (pp.40-41)

Say "80" and "40".
(pp.30-31)

TAXI, AUTOBÚS, Y METRO
Taxi, bus, and metro

The metro and some buses operate a ticket system where you have to validate your tickets in a machine. There's a standard fare per ride, but you can also buy a **metrobús**, a book of 10 tickets for both buses and metro.

2 Words to remember (4 minutes)

Familiarize yourself with these words.

el autobús *el aootoboos*	bus/coach
la taquilla *lah takeeyah*	ticket office
la estación de metro *lah estathyon day metroh*	metro station
la parada de autobús *lah paradah day aootoboos*	bus stop
la tarifa *lah tareefah*	fare
el taxi *el taksee*	taxi
la parada de taxis *lah paradah day taksees*	taxi rank

¿Para aquí el 17?
parah ahkee el deeaytheeseeaytay
Does the number 17 bus stop here?

3 In conversation: taxi (2 minutes)

A la Plaza de España, por favor.
ah lah plathah day espanyah, por fabor

Plaza de España, please.

Sí, de acuerdo, señor.
see, day akwairdo, senyor

Yes, certainly, sir.

¿Me puede dejar aquí, por favor?
may pweday dehar ahkee, por fabor

Can you drop me here, please?

4 Useful phrases (4 minutes)

Practise these phrases and then test yourself using the cover flap.

I'd like a taxi to go to the Prado.	**Quisiera un taxi para ir al Prado.** *keesyairah oon taksee parah eer al prado*
When is the next bus?	**¿Cuándo sale el próximo autobús?** *kwandoh salay el prokseemoh aootoboos*
How do you get to the museum?	**¿Cómo se va al museo?** *komoh say bah al moosayoh*
How long is the journey?	**¿Cuánto dura el viaje?** *kwantoh doorah el beeahay*
Please wait for me.	**Espéreme, por favor.** *esperemay, por fabor*

Cultural tip Metro lines in Madrid are known by numbers and the names of the first and last stations. Look out for the relevant end station. The Madrid metro runs every day between 6.00am and 2.00am.

6 Say it (2 minutes)

Do you go near the train station?

Do you go near the Prado?

When is the next bus to Barcelona?

5 In conversation: bus (2 minutes)

¿Pasa cerca del museo?
pasah therkah del moosayoh

Do you go near the museum?

Sí. Son 80 céntimos.
see. son ochentah thenteemos

Yes. That's 80 cents.

Avíseme cuando lleguemos.
abeesemay kwandoh yeghemos

Tell me when we arrive.

EN LA CARRETERA
On the road

Spanish **autopistas** (*motorways*) are fast but can be quite expensive. You will find signs for **el peaje** (*toll payment stations*). These have multiple lanes. Make sure you enter a green lane that allows payment by cash or credit card. Some lanes are for passholders or lorries only.

2 Match and repeat (4 minutes)

Match the numbered items to the list on the left, then test yourself.

❶ boot

❶ **el maletero**
   el malaytairoh

❷ **el parabrisas**
   el parabreesas

❸ **el capó**
   el kapoh

❹ **la rueda**
   lah rwedah

❺ **el neumático**
   el ne-oomateekoh

❻ **la puerta**
   lah pwertah

❼ **los faros**
   los faros

❽ **el parachoques**
   el parachokes

wheel ❹

tyre ❺

door ❻

Cultural tip Some self-service petrol stations can be unmanned. In this case, you usually have to specify how many litres you want and pay by card before filling up.

3 Road features (2 minutes)

la rotonda
lah rrotonduh

roundabout

el semáforo
el semaforoh

traffic lights

el cruce
el kroothay

intersection

4 Useful phrases (4 minutes)

Learn these phrases and then test yourself using the cover flap.

| The indicator doesn't work. | **El intermitente no funciona.** *el intairmeetaintay noh foonthyonah* |
| Fill it up, please. | **Lleno, por favor.** *yennoh, por fabor* |

② windscreen

③ bonnet

headlights ⑦ ⑧ bumper

5 Match and repeat (3 minutes)

Familiarize yourself with these words then test yourself using the flap.

petrol	**la gasolina** *lah gasoleenah*
diesel	**el gasoil** *el gasoil*
oil	**el aceite** *el ah-thayeetay*
engine	**el motor** *el motor*
gearbox	**la caja de cambios** *lah kahah day kambyos*
indicator	**el intermitente** *el intairmeetaintay*
flat tyre	**la rueda pinchada** *lah rwaydah peenchadah*
exhaust	**el tubo de escape** *el tooboh day eskapay*
driving licence	**el carné de conducir** *el karnay day kondootheer*

6 Say it (1 minute)

There's something wrong with my engine.

I have a flat tyre.

la autopista
lah aootopeestah

motorway/expressway

la autopista de peaje
lah aootopeestah day pyahay

toll motorway

el atasco de tráfico
el ataskoh day trafeekoh

traffic jam

REPASE Y REPITA
Review and repeat

1 Transport

1 el autobús
el aootoboos

2 el taxi
el taksee

3 el coche
el kochay

4 la bicicleta
lah beetheekletah

5 el metro
el metroh

1 Transport (3 minutes)

Name these forms of
transport in Spanish.

bus **1**

metro **5**

2 Go and take

1 ir
eer

2 cojo
kohoh

3 va
bah

4 vamos
bamos

5 cogen
kohen

6 voy
boy

2 Go and take (4 minutes)

Use the correct form of the verb in brackets.

1 Quiero ____ a la estación. (ir)

2 Yo ____ el metro. (coger)

3 ¿A dónde ____ usted? (ir)

4 Nosotros ____ al Museo del Prado. (ir)

5 Ellos ____ un taxi. (coger)

6 Yo ____ a Madrid. (ir)

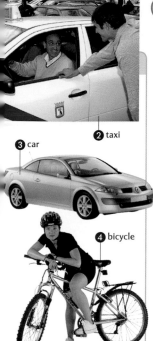

2 taxi

3 car

4 bicycle

3 You (4 minutes)

Use the correct form for **usted** or **tú** in each sentence.

❶ You are in a café. Ask "Do you have churros?"

❷ You are with a friend. Ask "Do you want a beer?"

❸ A visitor approaches you at your company reception. Ask "Do you have an appointment?"

❹ You are on the bus. Ask "Do you go near the station?"

❺ Ask your friend where she's going tomorrow.

4 Tickets (4 minutes)

You're buying tickets at a train station. Follow the conversation, replying in Spanish following the numbered English prompts.

¿Qué desea?
❶ I'd like two tickets to Sevilla.

¿De ida o de ida y vuelta?
❷ Return, please.

Muy bien. Cincuenta euros, por favor.
❸ What time does the train leave?

A las tres y diez.
❹ What platform does the train leave from?

Andén número siete.
❺ Thank you very much. Goodbye.

Respuestas
Answers (Cover with flap)

3 You

❶ ¿Tiene churros?
tyenay choorros

❷ ¿Quieres una cerveza?
kyaires oonah thairbaythah

❸ ¿Tiene una cita?
tyenay oonah theetah

❹ ¿Pasa cerca de la estación?
pasah therkah day lah estathyon

❺ ¿A dónde vas mañana?
ah donday bas manyanah

4 Tickets

❶ Quisiera dos billetes para Sevilla.
keesyairah dos beeyetes parah sebeeyah

❷ De ida y vuelta, por favor.
day eedah ee bweltah, por fabor

❸ ¿A qué hora sale el tren?
ah kay orah salay el tren

❹ ¿De qué andén sale el tren?
day kay anden salay el tren

❺ Muchas gracias. Adiós.
moochas grathyas. addy-os

EN LA CIUDAD
About town

1 Warm up (1 minute)

Ask "How do you get to the museum?" (pp.42-3)

Say "I want to take the metro" and "I don't want to take a taxi". (pp.40-1)

Note that the Spanish word **museo** (*museum*) also means art gallery when it's a public building in which works of art are exhibited; **galería de arte** usually refers to a shop that sells works of art. Be careful, too, not to confuse **librería** (*bookshop* or *bookshelf*) and **biblioteca** (*library*).

2 Match and repeat (4 minutes)

Match the numbered locations to the words in the panel.

❶ el ayuntamiento
el ahyoonta-myaintoh

❷ el puente
el pwentay

❸ el centro
el thentroh

❹ la iglesia
lah eegleseeah

❺ la plaza
lah plathah

❻ el aparcamiento
el aparka-myaintoh

❼ la biblioteca
lah bibleeotekah

❽ el museo
el moosayoh

❶ town hall   church ❹

city centre ❸

❺ square

3 Words to remember (3 minutes)

Familiarize yourself with these words and test yourself using the cover flap.

la gasolinera *lah gasoleenerah*	petrol station
la oficina de información turística *lah ohfeetheenah day eenformathyon tooreesteekah*	tourist information
la piscina municipal *lah pistheenah mooneetheepal*	public swimming pool

❼ library

Conversational tip In Spanish there are two ways of saying *am*, *is*, or *are*. You have already learned the verb **ser** (p.14): **soy inglés** (*I am English*); **es vegetariano** (*he is vegetarian*). When talking about where something is, you need to use a different verb: **estar**. The most important forms of this verb are: **estoy** (*I am*), **está** (*he/she/it is*), and **están** (*they are*): **¿Dónde están lla iglesia?** (*Where is the church?*); **El café no está lejos.** (*The café isn't far.*)

4 Useful phrases (4 minutes)

Practise these phrases and then test yourself using the cover flap.

Is there an art gallery in town?	**¿Hay algún museo de arte en la ciudad?** ah-ee algoon moosayoh day artay en lah thyoodad
Is it far from here?	**¿Está lejos de aquí?** estah lehos day ahkee
There is a swimming pool near the bridge.	**Hay una piscina cerca del puente.** ah-ee oonah peestheenah therkah del pwentay

La catedral está en el centro. lah katedral estah en el thentroh The cathedral is in the city centre.

5 Put into practice (3 minutes)

bridge ②

Join in this conversation. Read the Spanish on the left and follow the instructions to make your reply. Then test yourself.

¿Le puedo ayudar? lay pwedoh ahyoodar

Can I help you?

Ask: Is there a library in town?

¿Hay alguna biblioteca en la ciudad? ah-ee algoonah beebleeotekah en lah thyoodad

car park ⑥

No, pero hay un museo. noh, peroh ah-ee oon moosayoh

No, but there's a museum.

Ask: How do I get to the museum?

¿Cómo se va al museo? komoh say bah al moosayoh

museum ⑧

Está por allí. estah por ahyee

It's over there.

Say: Thank you very much.

Muchas gracias. moochas grathyas

LAS DIRECCIONES
Directions

1 Warm up (1 minute)

How do you say "near the station"? (pp.42-3)

Say "Take the first on the left". (pp.40-1)

Ask "Where are you going?" (pp.40-1)

You'll often be able to find a **plano de la ciudad** (*town map*) in the town centre, usually near the town hall or tourist office. In the older parts of Spanish towns there are often narrow streets, where you will usually find a one-way system in operation. Parking is usually restricted.

2 Useful phrases (4 minutes)

el bloque de oficinas
el blokay day ohfeetheenas
office block

Learn these phrases and then test yourself.

Tuerza a la izquierda/ derecha. *twerthah ah lah eethkyairdah/derechah*	Turn left/right.
todo recto *todoh rrektoh*	straight on
¿Cómo se va a la piscina? *komoh say bah ah lah peestheenah*	How do I get to the swimming pool?
la primera a la derecha *lah preemerah ah lah derechah*	first right
la segunda a la izquierda *lah segoondah ah lah eethkyairdah*	second left

la fuente
lah fwentay
fountain

3 In conversation (4 minutes)

¿Hay un restaurante en la ciudad?
ah-ee oon restaoorantay en la thyoodad

Is there a restaurant nearby?

Sí, cerca de la estación.
see, therkah day lah estathyon

Yes, near the station.

¿Cómo se va a la estación?
komoh say bah ah lah estathyon

How do I get to the station?

4 Words to remember (4 minutes)

Me he perdido.
may eh perdeedoh
I'm lost.

el centro deportivo
el thentroh deporteeboh
leisure centre

Familiarize yourself with these words and test
yourself using the flap.

traffic lights	**el semáforo** *el semaforoh*
corner	**la esquina** *lah eskeenah*
street/road	**la calle** *lah kayay*
main road	**la calle principal** *lah kayay preentheepal*
at the end of the street	**al final de la calle** *al feenal day lah kayay*
map	**el plano** *el planoh*
flyover	**el paso elevado** *el pasoh elebadoh*
opposite	**enfrente de** *enfrentay day*

la zona peatonal
lah thonah pe-ahtonal
pedestrian zone

¿Dondé estamos?
donday estamos
Where are we?

5 Say it (2 minutes)

Turn right at the end
of the street.

Turn left opposite
the museum.

It's ten minutes by bus.

**Tuerza a la izquierda en
el semáforo.**
*twerthah ah lah
eethkyairdah en el semaforoh*

Turn left at the traffic lights.

¿Está lejos?
estah lehos

Is it far?

**No, cinco minutos
andando.**
*noh, theenkoh meenootos
andandoh*

No, it's five minutes
on foot.

1 Warm up (1 minute)

Say the days of the week in Spanish. (pp.28-9)

How do you say "six o'clock"? (pp.30-1)

Ask "What time is it?" (pp.30-1)

EL TURISMO
Sightseeing

Most national museums and art galleries close on Mondays and public holidays. Although shops are normally closed on Sundays, many will open in tourist areas. In provincial areas, it is not unusual for public buildings and shops to close at lunchtime, between 1.30 and 4.30pm.

2 Words to remember (4 minutes)

Familiarize yourself with these words and test yourself using the flap.

la guía *lah gheeah*	guidebook
la entrada *lah entradah*	entrance ticket
el horario de apertura *el oraryoh day apertoorah*	opening times
el día festivo *el deeyah festeevoh*	public holiday
entrada libre *entradah leebray*	free entrance

la visita con guía
lah beeseetah kon gheeah
guided tour

Cultural tip If a public holiday falls on a Thursday or a Tuesday, people will often **hacer puente** (do a bridge) - in other words, they take Friday or Monday off as well, to make a long weekend.

3 In conversation (3 minutes)

¿Abren esta tarde?
ahbren estah tarday

Do you open
this afternoon?

**Sí, pero cerramos a
las cuatro.**
*see, peroh therramos ah las
kwatroh*

Yes, but we close at
four o'clock.

**¿Tienen acceso para sillas
de ruedas?**
*tyenen akthesoh parah
seeyas day rwedas*

Do you have access
for wheelchairs?

4 Useful phrases (3 minutes)

Practise these phrases and then test yourself using the cover flap.

What time do you open/close?	**¿A qué hora abre/cierra?** ah kay _orah_ _ah_bray/ th_yairr_ah
Where are the toilets?	**¿Dónde están los servicios?** _don_day es_tan_ los serbeethyos
Is there access for wheelchairs?	**¿Hay acceso para sillas de ruedas?** ah-ee ak_thes_oh _par_ah _see_yas day _rwe_das

5 Put into practice (4 minutes)

Cover the text on the right and complete the dialogue in Spanish.

Lo siento, el museo está cerrado.
loh _syen_toh, el moosayoh es_tah_ therradoh

Sorry. The museum is closed.

Ask: Do you open on Tuesdays?

¿Abren los martes?
_ah_bren los _mar_tes

Sí, pero cerramos temprano.
see, _per_oh ther_ra_mos tem_pra_noh

Yes, but we close early.

Ask: At what time?

¿A qué hora?
ah kay _or_ah

Sí, el ascensor está allí.
see, el asthen_sor_ es_tah_ ah-_yee_

Yes, there's a lift over there.

Gracias, quisiera cuatro entradas.
grathyas, kees_yai_rah _kwa_troh en_tra_das

Thank you, I'd like four entrance tickets.

Aquí tiene, y la guía es gratis.
ah_kee_ tyenay, ee lah _ghee_ah es _gra_tees

Here you are, and the guidebook is free.

1 **Warm up** (1 minute)

Say "half past one".
(pp.30-1)

What's the Spanish for
"ticket"? (pp.38-9)

Say "I am going to New
York". (pp.40-1)

EN EL AEROPUERTO
At the airport

Although the airport environment is largely
international, it is sometimes useful to be able to
ask your way around the terminal in Spanish. It's a
good idea to make sure you have a few coins when
you arrive at the airport; you may need to pay for
a luggage trolley.

2 **Words to remember** (4 minutes)

Familiarize yourself with these words and
test yourself using the flap.

la facturación *lah faktoorathyon*	check-in
las salidas *las saleedas*	departures
las llegadas *las yehgadas*	arrivals
la aduana *lah adwanah*	customs
el control de pasaportes *el kontrol day pasaportes*	passport control
la terminal *lah termeenal*	terminal
la puerta de embarque *lah pwertah day embarkay*	boarding gate

**¿Cuál es la puerta de embarque
para el vuelo veintitrés?**
*kwal es lah pwertah day embarkay
parah el bweloh bayeenteetres*
Which is the boarding gate
for flight 23?

3 **Useful phrases** (3 minutes)

Learn these phrases and then test yourself
using the cover flap.

¿Sale a su hora el vuelo para Sevilla? *salay ah soo orah el bweloh parah seveeyah*	Is the flight for Seville on time?
No encuentro mi equipaje. *noh enkwentroh mee ehkeepahay*	I can't find my luggage.

4 Put into practice (3 minutes)

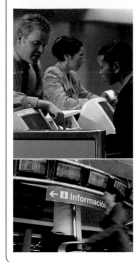

Join in this conversation. Read the Spanish on the left and follow the instructions to make your reply. Then test yourself by concealing the answers using the cover flap.

Hola, ¿le puedo ayudar?
o-lah, lay pwedoh ahyoodar

Hello, can I help you?

Ask: Is the flight to Madrid on time?

¿Sale a su hora el vuelo para Madrid?
salay ah soo orah el bweloh parah madreed

Sí señor.
see senyor

Yes sir.

Ask: Which is the boarding gate?

¿Cuál es la puerta de embarque?
kwal es lah pwertah day embarkay

5 Match and repeat (4 minutes)

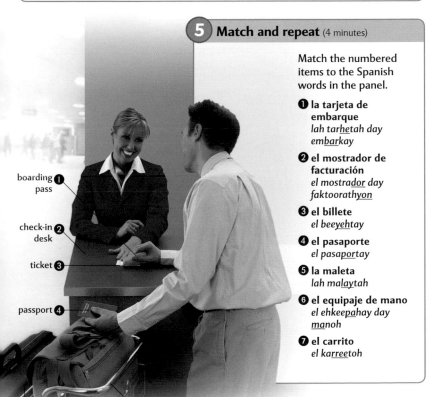

Match the numbered items to the Spanish words in the panel.

❶ **la tarjeta de embarque**
lah tarhetah day embarkay

❷ **el mostrador de facturación**
el mostrador day faktoorathyon

❸ **el billete**
el beeyehtay

❹ **el pasaporte**
el pasaportay

❺ **la maleta**
lah malaytah

❻ **el equipaje de mano**
el ehkeepahay day manoh

❼ **el carrito**
el karreetoh

boarding pass ❶

check-in desk ❷

ticket ❸

passport ❹

❼ trolley

❺ suitcase   ❻ hand luggage

REPASE Y REPITA
Review and repeat

Respuestas
Answers (Cover with flap)

1 Places

❶ **el museo**
el moosayoh

❷ **el ayuntamiento**
el ahyoonta-myaintoh

❸ **el puente**
el pwentay

❹ **la biblioteca**
lah beeblee-ohtekah

❺ **el aparcamiento**
el ahparka-myaintoh

❻ **la catedral**
lah katedral

❼ **la plaza**
lah plathah

1 Places (4 minutes)

Name the numbered places in Spanish.

❶ museum

❷ town hall

❸ bridge

❹ library

❺ car park

❻ cathedral

square ❼

2 Car parts

❶ **el parabrisas**
el parabreesas

❷ **el intermitente**
el intairmee-taintay

❸ **el capó**
el kapoh

❹ **el neumático**
el ne-oomateekoh

❺ **la puerta**
lah pwertah

❻ **el parachoques**
el parachokes

2 Car parts (3 minutes)

Name these car parts in Spanish.

windscreen ❶

❹ tyre

❺ door

3 Questions (4 minutes)

Ask the questions that match these answers.

❶ **El autobús sale a las ocho.**
el aootoboos salay ah las ochoh

❷ **El café es un euro cincuenta.**
el kafay es oon eh-ooro theenkwentah

❸ **No, no quiero vino.**
noh, noh kyairoh beenoh

❹ **El tren sale del andén cinco.**
el tren salay del anden theenkoh

❺ **Nosotros vamos a León.**
nosotros bamos ah leh-on

❻ **El próximo tren es dentro de quince minutos.**
el prokseemoh tren es dentroh day keenthay meenootos

3 Questions

❶ **¿A qué hora sale el autobús?**
ah kay orah salay el aootoboos

❷ **¿Cuánto es el café?**
kwantoh es el kafay

❸ **¿Quieres vino?**
kyaires beenoh

❹ **¿De qué andén sale el tren?**
day kay anden salay el tren

❺ **¿A dónde vais?**
ah donday baees

❻ **¿Cuándo es el próximo tren?**
kwandoh es el prokseemoh tren

4 Verbs (4 minutes)

 indicator

 bonnet

bumper

Choose the correct form of the verb in brackets to fill the gaps.

❶ **Yo ____ inglés. (ser)**

❷ **Nosotros ____ el metro. (tomar)**

❸ **Ella ____ a Marbella. (ir)**

❹ **Él ____ casado. (estar)**

❺ **¿Tú ____ un té? (querer)**

❻ **¿Cuántos niños ____ usted? (tener)**

4 Verbs

❶ **soy**
soy

❷ **cogemos**
kohaymos

❸ **va**
bah

❹ **está**
estah

❺ **quieres**
kyaires

❻ **tiene**
tyenay

1 Warm up (1 minute)

Ask "Do you accept credit cards?" (pp.38-9)

Ask "How much is that?" (pp.18-19)

Ask "Do you have children?" (pp.10-11)

RESERVAR UNA HABITACIÓN
Booking a room

Types of accommodation in Spain include: **hotel**, categorized from one to five stars; **pensión**, a small family-run hotel; **hostal**, cheap and basic; and **parador**, state-owned hotels in historic properties or places of great beauty.

2 Useful phrases (3 minutes)

Practise these phrases and then test yourself by concealing the Spanish on the left using the cover flap.

¿El desayuno está incluido? *el desayoonoh estah inklooeedoh*	Is breakfast included?

¿Aceptan animales de compañía? *atheptan aneemales day kompanyeeah*	Do you accept pets?

¿Tienen servicio de habitaciones? *tyenen serbeethyoh day abeetathyones*	Do you have room service?

¿A qué hora tengo que dejar la habitación? *ah kay orah tengoh kay dehar lah abeetathyon*	What time do I have to leave the room?

3 In conversation (5 minutes)

¿Tiene habitaciones libres?
tyenay abeetathyones leebres

Do you have any vacancies?

Sí, una habitación doble.
see, oonah abeetathyon doblay

Yes, a double room.

¿Tiene una cuna?
tyenay oonah koonah

Do you have a cot?

4 Words to remember (4 minutes)

Familiarize yourself with these words and test yourself by concealing the Spanish on the right using the cover flap.

¿Tiene la habitación vistas al parque?
tyenay lah abeetathyon beestas al parkay
Does the room have a view over the park?

room	**la habitación** *lah abeetathyon*
single room	**la habitación individual** *lah abeetathyon indeebeedwal*
double room	**la habitación doble** *lah abeetathyon doblay*
bathroom	**el cuarto de baño** *el kwartoh day banyoh*
shower	**la ducha** *lah doochah*
breakfast	**el desayuno** *el desayoonoh*
key	**la llave** *lah yabay*
balcony	**el balcón** *el balkon*
air-conditioning	**el aire acondicionado** *el ah-eeray akondeethyonadoh*

5 Say it (2 minutes)

Do you have a single room, please?

For six nights.

Is breakfast included?

Cultural tip Large hotels and **paradors** are generally the only types of hotel to offer breakfast, but you will generally be charged extra for it. If your accommodation doesn't provide breakfast, you'll usually find it easy to discover a bar or a café nearby where you can go for **café con leche** in the mornings.

Sí, claro. ¿Cuántas noches?
see, klaroh. kwantas noches

Yes, of course. How many nights?

Para tres noches.
parah tres noches

For three nights.

Muy bien. Aquí tiene la llave.
mwee byen. ahkee tyenay lah yabay

Very good. Here's the key.

EN EL HOTEL
In the hotel

1 Warm up (1 minute)

Say "Is there...?" and "There isn't...". (pp.48-9)

What does "¿Le puedo ayudar?" mean? (pp.54-5)

Although the larger hotels almost always have en-suite bathrooms, there are still some **pensiones** and **hostales** where you will have to share bathroom facilities and which usually don't provide towels. It is always advisable to check what is provided when you book.

2 Match and repeat (6 minutes)

Match the numbered items in this hotel bedroom with the Spanish text in the panel and test yourself using the cover flap.

❶ la mesilla de noche
lah meseeyah day nochay

❷ la lámpara
lah lamparah

❸ el minibar
el meeneebar

❹ las cortinas
las korteenas

❺ el sofá
el sofah

❻ la almohada
lah almoh-ahdah

❼ el cojín
el koheen

❽ la cama
lah kamah

❾ la colcha
lah kolchah

❿ la manta
lah mantah

❶ bedside table
❷ lamp
❸ minibar
❹ curtains
❺ sofa
❻ pillow
❼ cushion
❽ bed
❾ bedspread
❿ blanket

Cultural tip When you arrive in your double room, you will usually see one long pillow instead of two individual ones on the bed. This is the usual pillow for a double bed – **cama de matrimonio** (literally, *marriage bed*). If you don't want to share your bed or pillow, you'll have to ask for **una habitación doble con dos camas** (*a double room with two beds*) to get a twin room.

3 Useful phrases (5 minutes)

Practise these phrases and then test yourself using the cover flap.

The room is too cold/hot. **Hace demasiado frío/ calor en la habitación.** *ahthay daymasyahdoh freeoh/kalor en lah abeetathyon*

There are no towels. **No hay toallas.** *noh ah-ee toh-ahyas*

I need some soap. **Necesito jabón.** *netheseetoh habon*

The shower doesn't work. **La ducha no funciona.** *lah doochah noh foonthyonah*

The lift is broken. **El ascensor está roto.** *el asthensor estah rrotoh*

4 Put into practice (3 minutes)

Practise these phrases and then complete the dialogue in Spanish.

¿Le atienden? *lay atyainden*

Can I help you?

Say: I need some pillows.

Necesito almohadas. *netheseetoh almoh-ahdas*

La camarera se las llevará. *lah kamarairah say las yebarah*

The maid will bring some.

Say: And the TV doesn't work.

Y la televisión no funciona. *ee lah telebeesyon noh foonthyonah*

EN EL CÁMPING
At the campsite

1 Warm up (1 minute)

How do you ask "Can I?" (pp.34-5)

Say "The lift is broken". (pp.60-1)

Say "I need some towels". (pp.60-1)

Camping is very popular in Spain. The country's numerous campsites are well organized and operate on a star system. The local tourist information office will be able to offer a list of campsites in the area together with their ratings. It is advisable to book in advance during the summer months.

2 Useful phrases (3 minutes)

Learn these phrases and then test yourself by concealing the Spanish with the cover flap.

¿Puedo alquilar una bicicleta? *pwedoh alkeelar oonah beetheekletah*	Can I rent a bicycle?
¿Es el agua potable? *es el ahgwah potablay*	Is this drinking water?
¿Se permiten hogueras? *say permeeten ohgheras*	Are campfires allowed?
Las radios están prohibidas. *las rradyos estan proheebeedas*	Radios are forbidden.

¿Dónde está el grifo?
donday estah el greefoh
Where is the tap?

la oficina
lah ofeetheenah
office

el contenedor de la basura
el kontenedor day lah basoorah
litter bin

el doble techo
el doblay taychoh
fly sheet

3 In conversation (5 minutes)

Necesito una plaza para tres noches.
netheseetoh oonah plathah parah tres noches

I need a pitch for three nights.

Hay una cerca de la piscina.
ah-ee oonah therkah day lah peestheenah

There's one near the swimming pool.

¿Cuánto cuesta para una roulotte?
kwantoh kwestah parah oonah rroolot

How much is it for a caravan?

5 Say it (2 minutes)

I need a pitch for four nights.

Can I rent a tent?

Where's the electrical hook-up?

los aseos
los asayos
toilets

el punto de luz
el poontoh day looth
electrical hook-up

la cuerda
lah kwerdah
guy rope

la clavija
la klabeehah
tent peg

4 Words to remember (4 minutes)

Learn these words and then test yourself using the cover flap.

campsite	**el cámping** *el kampeen*
tent	**la tienda** *lah tyendah*
caravan	**la roulotte** *lah rroolot*
camper van	**la autocaravana** *la ah-ootokarabanah*
pitch	**la plaza** *lah plathah*
campfire	**la hoguera** *lah ohgherah*
drinking water	**el agua potable** *el ahgwah potablay*
rubbish	**la basura** *lah basoorah*
camping gas	**el camping-gas** *el kampeen gas*
showers	**las duchas** *las doochas*
sleeping bag	**el saco de dormir** *el sakoh day dormeer*
air mattress	**la colchoneta** *lah kolchonetah*
ground sheet	**el suelo aislante** *el sweloh ah-eeslantay*

Cincuenta euros. Una noche por adelantado.
theenkwentah eh-ooros. oonah nochay por adelantadoh

Fifty euros. One night in advance.

¿Puedo alquilar una barbacoa?
pwedoh alkeelar oonah barbakoh-ah

Can I rent a barbecue?

Sí, pero tiene que dejar una señal.
see, peroh tyenay kay dehar oonah senyal

Yes, but you must pay a deposit.

DESCRIPCIONES
Descriptions

Adjectives are words used to describe things. In Spanish you generally put the adjective after the thing it describes in the same gender and number: **una bebida fría** (*a cold drink*, feminine singular); **un café frío** (*a cold coffee*, masculine singular); **dos bebidas frías** (*two cold drinks*, feminine plural).

2   Words to remember (7 minutes)

Adjectives change depending on whether the thing described is masculine (**el**) or feminine (**la**). Generally, a final **o** changes to **a** in the feminine, but if the adjective ends with **e** (such as **grande**) it doesn't change for the feminine. To form the plural, just add an **s**.

duro/dura *dooroh/doorah*	hard
blando/blanda *blandoh/blandah*	soft
caliente *kalyaintay*	hot
frío/fría *freeoh/freeah*	cold
grande *granday*	big
pequeño/pequeña *pekenyoh/pekenyah*	small
bonito/bonita *boneetoh/boneetah*	beautiful
feo/fea *feh-oh/feh-ah*	ugly
ruidoso/ruidosa *rrweedosoh/rrweedosah*	noisy
tranquilo/tranquila *trankeeloh/trankeelah*	quiet
bueno/buena *bwenoh/bwenah*	good
malo/mala *maloh/malah*	bad
lento/lenta *lentoh/lentah*	slow
rápido/rápida *rrapeedoh/rrapeedah*	fast

las montañas altas
 las montanyas altas
 high mountains

la tienda pequeña
 lah tyaindah pekenyah
 small shop

el coche viejo
 el koche bee-ayhoh
 old car

El pueblo es muy bonito.
 el pwebloh es mwee boneetoh
 The village is very beautiful.

la calle tranquila
 lah kayay trankeelah
 quiet road

3 Useful phrases (4 minutes)

Learn these phrases. Note that you can emphasize a description by using **muy** (*very*), **demasiado** (*too*), or **más** (*more*) before the adjective.

| This coffee is cold. | **Este café está frío.**
estay kafay estah free-oh |
|---|---|

| My room is very noisy. | **Mi habitación es muy ruidosa.**
mee abeetathyon es mwee rrweedosah |
|---|---|

| My car is too small. | **Mi coche es demasiado pequeño.**
mee koche es demasyahdoh pekenyoh |
|---|---|

| I need a softer bed. | **Necesito una cama más blanda.**
netheseetoh oonah kamah mas blandah |
|---|---|

4 Put into practice (3 minutes)

Join in this conversation. Cover up the text on the right and complete the dialogue in Spanish. Check and repeat if necessary.

Ésta es la habitación.
estah es lah abeetathyon
This is the bedroom.
Say: The view is very beautiful.

La vista es muy bonita.
lah beestah es mwee boneetah

El cuarto de baño está por ahí.
el kwartoh day banyoh estah por ah-ee
The bathroom is over there.
Say: It is too small.

Es demasiado pequeño.
es demasyahdoh pekenyoh

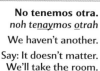

No tenemos otra.
noh tenaymos otrah
We haven't another.
Say: It doesn't matter. We'll take the room.

No importa. Nos quedamos con la habitación.
noh importah. nos kedamos kon lah abeetathyon

REPASE Y REPITA
Review and repeat

1 Descriptions

❶ **caliente**
kalyaintay

❷ **pequeña**
pekenyah

❸ **frío**
free-oh

❹ **grande**
granday

❺ **tranquila**
trankeelah

1 Descriptions (3 minutes)

Put the word in brackets into Spanish. Use the correct masculine or feminine form.

❶ El agua está demasiado _____. (hot)

❷ La cama es muy _____. (small)

❸ El café está _____. (cold)

❹ Este cuarto de baño es más _____. (big)

❺ Quisiera una habitación más _____. (quiet)

2 Campsite

❶ **el punto de luz**
el poontoh day looth

❷ **la tienda**
lah tyaindah

❸ **el contenedor de la basura**
el kontenedor day lah basoorah

❹ **la cuerda**
lah kwerdah

❺ **los aseos**
los asayos

❻ **la roulotte**
lah rroolot

2 Campsite (3 minutes)

Name these items you might find in a campsite.

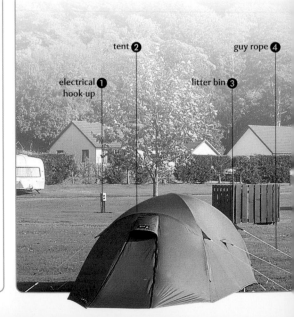

tent ❷

guy rope ❹

electrical ❶
hook-up

litter bin ❸

Respuestas
Answers (Cover with flap)

3 At the hotel (4 minutes)

You are booking a room in a hotel. Follow the conversation, replying in Spanish where you can see the English prompts.

¿Qué desean?
❶ Do you have any vacancies?

Sí, una habitación doble.
❷ Do you accept pets?

Sí. ¿Cuántas noches?
❸ Three nights.

Son ciento cuarenta euros.
❹ Is breakfast included?

Sí. Aquí tiene la llave.
❺ Thank you very much.

3 At the hotel

❶ **¿Tiene habitaciones libres?**
tyenay abeeta-thyones leebres

❷ **¿Aceptan animales de compañía?**
atheptan aneemales day kompanyeeah

❸ **Tres noches.**
tres noches

❹ **¿El desayuno está incluido?**
el desayoonoh estah inklooeedoh

❺ **Muchas gracias.**
moochas grathyas

4 Negatives (5 minutes)

Make these sentences negative using the verb in brackets.

❶ Yo _____ hijos. (tener)
❷ Ellos _____ a Madrid mañana. (ir)
❸ Él _____ un café. (querer)
❹ Yo _____ el metro. (coger)
❺ La vista _____ muy bonita. (ser)

4 Negatives

❶ **no tengo**
noh tengoh
❷ **no van**
noh ban
❸ **no quiere**
noh kyairay
❹ **no cojo**
noh kohoh
❺ **no es**
no es

❺ toilets

❻ caravan

DE COMPRAS
Shopping

1 Warm up (1 minute)

Ask "How do I get to the station?" (pp.50–1)

Say "Turn left at the traffic lights" and "The station is opposite the café". (pp.50–1)

Small, traditional shops are still very common in Spain. But you can also find big supermarkets and shopping centres on the outskirts of cities. Local markets selling fresh, local produce can be found everywhere. Find out the market day from the **oficina de información turística** (*tourist office*).

2 Match and repeat (5 minutes)

Match the shops numbered 1 to 9 below and right to the Spanish in the panel. Then test yourself using the cover flap.

❶ la panadería
 lah panadaire<u>ee</u>ah

❷ la pastelería
 lah pastaylaire<u>ee</u>ah

❸ el estanco
 el est<u>a</u>nkoh

❹ la carnicería
 lah karnee-thaire<u>ee</u>ah

❺ la charcutería
 lah charkoo-taire<u>ee</u>ah

❻ la librería
 lah leebraire<u>ee</u>ah

❼ la pescadería
 lah peskadaire<u>ee</u>ah

❽ la joyería
 la hoyere<u>ee</u>ah

❾ el banco
 el <u>ban</u>koh

❶ baker

❷ cake shop

❹ butcher

❺ delicatessen

❼ fishmonger

❽ jeweller

Conversational tip If you want an everyday bar of soap or a tube of toothpaste, you need to go to a **droguería** (*drugstore*) rather than the **farmacia** (*pharmacy*). The **estanco** (*tobacconist*) is the place for all sorts of tobacco products and stamps. **Papelerías** cater for all your stationery needs. Most Spanish shops offer a free gift-wrapping service; you only need to ask: "**¿Me lo envuelve para regalo?**" (*May I have it gift-wrapped?*).

¿Dónde está la floristería?
donday estah lah floreestaireeah
Where is the florist?

❸ tobacconist

❻ bookshop

❾ bank

❸ Words to remember (4 minutes)

Familiarize yourself with these words and test yourself using the cover flap.

hardware shop	**la ferretería** *lah ferretaireeah*
antique shop	**el anticuario** *el anteekwareeoh*
hairdresser	**la peluquería** *lah pelookaireeah*
greengrocer	**la verdulería** *lah berdoolaireeah*
post office	**la oficina de correos** *lah ofeetheenah* *day korrayos*
shoe shop	**la zapatería** *lah thapataireeah*
dry cleaner	**la tintorería** *lah teentoraireeah*
grocer	**el ultramarinos** *el ooltramareenos*

❹ Useful phrases (3 minutes)

Familiarize yourself with these phrases.

Where is the hairdresser?	**¿Dónde está la peluquería?** *donday estah* *lah pelookaireeah*
Where do I pay?	**¿Dónde se paga?** *donday say pagah*
I'm just looking, thank you.	**Sólo estoy mirando, gracias.** *soloh estoy meerandoh grathyas*
Do you sell SIM cards?	**¿Tiene tarjetas SIM?** *tyenay tarhetas seem*
May I have two of those?	**¿Me pone dos de éstos?** *may ponay dos day estos*
Can I place an order?	**¿Puedo hacer un pedido?** *pwedoh ahther oon pedeedoh*

❺ Say it (2 minutes)

Where is the bank?

Do you sell cheese?

Where do I pay?

EN EL MERCADO
At the market

1 **Warm up** (1 minute)

What is Spanish for "40", "56", "77", "82", and "94"? (pp.10-11 and pp.30-1)

Say "I'd like a big room". (pp.64-5)

Ask "Do you have a small car?" (pp.64-5)

Spain uses the metric system of weights and measures. You need to ask for the produce in kilogrammes or grammes. Some larger items, such as melons or pineapples, tend to be sold as **la pieza** (as single items); other items, such as lettuce, may be sold in lots of two or three.

2 **Match and repeat** (4 minutes)

Match the numbered items in this scene with the text in the panel.

1 **los tomates**
los to*mates*

2 **las judías**
las hoo*dee*as

3 **los champiñones**
los champeen*yo*nes

4 **las uvas**
las *oo*bas

5 **los pepinos**
los pe*pee*nos

6 **las alcachofas**
las alka*cho*fas

7 **los guisantes**
los ghee*san*tes

8 **los pimientos**
los peem*yain*tos

1 tomatoes

8 peppers

5 cucumbers

6 artichokes

7 peas

3 **In conversation:** (3 minutes)

Quisiera tomates.
kees*yair*ah to*mates*

I'd like some tomatoes.

¿De los grandes o de los pequeños?
day los *gran*des oh day los pe*ken*yos

The large ones or the small ones?

Dos kilos de los pequeños, por favor.
dos *kee*los day los pe*ken*yos, por *fa*bor

Two kilos of the small ones, please.

Cultural tip Spain uses the common European currency, the euro, which is divided into 100 **centimos**. Spanish-speaking countries in Central and South America all have their own currencies. Argentina, Chile, Uruguay, Colombia, and México all call their currency the **peso**, which is divided into 100 **centavos**.

grapes **4**
mushrooms **3**
beans **2**

4 Useful phrases (5 minutes)

Practise these phrases and then test yourself using the cover flap.

Esa salchicha es demasiado cara.
ehsah salcheechah es demasyahdoh karah

That sausage is too expensive.

¿A cuánto está esa?
ah kwantoh estah ehsa

How much is that one?

5 Say it (2 minutes)

Two kilos of peas, please.

The mushrooms are too expensive.

How much are the grapes?

Eso es todo.
ehsoh es todoh

That'll be all.

¿Algo más, señorita?
algoh mas, senyoreetah

Anything else, miss?

**Eso es todo, gracias.
¿Cuánto es?**
*ehsoh es todoh, grathyas.
kwantoh es*

That'll be all, thank you.
How much?

Tres cincuenta.
tres theenkwentah

Three fifty.

1 Warm up (1 minute)

What are these items you could buy in a supermarket? (pp.24–5)

la carne
el pescado
el queso
el zumo
el vino
el agua

EN EL SUPERMERCADO
At the supermarket

Prices in supermarkets are usually lower than in smaller shops. They offer all kinds of products, with the larger out-of-town **hipermercados** offering clothes, household goods, garden furniture, and DIY products.

2 Match and repeat (5 minutes)

Look at the numbered product categories and match them to the Spanish words in the panel on the left.

❶ **los productos del hogar**
los prodooktos del ohgar

❷ **la fruta**
lah frootah

❸ **las bebidas**
las bebeedas

❹ **los platos preparados**
los platos preparados

❺ **los productos de belleza**
los prodooktos day beyethah

❻ **los productos lácteos**
los prodooktos lakteh-os

❼ **la verdura**
lah berdoorah

❽ **los congelados**
los konhelados

household ❶ products

fruit ❷

drinks ❸

ready meals ❹

vegetables ❼

frozen foods ❽

Cultural tip You cannot usually take unweighed fruit and vegetables sold by the kilo straight to the check-out at a supermarket. There is usually a separate counter or a self-service weighing machine.

3 Useful phrases (3 minutes)

Learn these phrases and then test yourself using the cover flap.

May I have a bag, please?	**¿Me da una bolsa, por favor?** *may dah oonah bolsah, por fabor*
Where are the drinks?	**¿Dónde están las bebidas?** *donday estan las bebeedas*
Where is the check-out, please?	**¿Dónde está la caja, por favor?** *donday estah lah kahah, por fabor*
Please key in your PIN.	**Por favor, meta su PIN.** *por fabor, metah soo peen*

❺ beauty products

❻ dairy products

4 Words to remember (4 minutes)

Learn these words and then test yourself using the cover flap.

bread	**el pan** *el pan*
milk	**la leche** *lah lechay*
butter	**la mantequilla** *lah mantekeeyah*
ham	**el jamón** *el hamon*
salt	**la sal** *lah sal*
pepper	**la pimienta** *lah peemyaintah*
washing powder	**el jabón de lavadora** *el habon day labadorah*
toilet paper	**el papel higiénico** *el papel eehyaineekoh*
nappies	**los pañales** *los panyales*

5 Say it (2 minutes)

Where are the dairy products?

May I have some cheese, please?

Where are the frozen foods?

LA ROPA Y LOS ZAPATOS
Clothes and shoes

Clothes and shoes are measured in metric sizes from 36 upwards. Even allowing for conversion of sizes, Spanish clothes tend to be cut smaller than English ones. Clothes size is **la talla**, but shoe size is **el número**.

2 Match and repeat (3 minutes)

Match the numbered items of clothing to the Spanish words in the panel on the left. Test yourself using the cover flap.

1 la camisa
lah kameesah

2 la corbata
lah korbatah

3 la chaqueta
lah chaketah

4 el bolsillo
el bolseeyoh

5 la manga
lah mangah

6 el pantalón
el pantalon

7 la falda
lah faldah

8 las medias
las medyas

9 los zapatos
los thapatos

shirt 1
tie 2
jacket 3
pocket 4
sleeve 5
trousers 6

Cultural tip As in most of mainland Europe, Spain uses the continental system of sizes. Women's clothes sizes usually range from 36 (UK 8, US 6) through to 46 (UK 20, US 18), and shoe sizes from 37 (UK 4, US 5½) to 45 (UK 11, US 12). For men's shirts, a size 41 is a 16-inch collar, 43 is a 17-inch collar, and 45 is an 18-inch collar.

3 Useful phrases (5 minutes)

Practise these phrases and then test yourself using the cover flap.

Do you have a larger size?	**¿Tiene una talla más grande?** *tyenay oonah tayah mas granday*
It's not what I want.	**No es lo que quiero.** *noh es loh kay kyairoh*
I'll take the pink one.	**Me quedo con el rosa.** *may kedoh kon el rrosah*

4 Words to remember (4 minutes)

Colours are adjectives (pp.64–5) and in most cases have a masculine and a feminine form. The feminine is usually formed by substituting an **a** for the final **o**.

red	**rojo/roja** *rrohoh/rrohah*
white	**blanco/blanca** *blankoh/blankah*
blue	**azul** *athool*
yellow	**amarillo/amarilla** *amareeyoh/amareeyah*
green	**verde** *berday*
black	**negro/negra** *negroh/negrah*

7 skirt

8 tights

9 shoes

5 Say it (2 minutes)

What shoe size?

Do you have a black jacket?

Do you have size 38?

Do you have a smaller size?

REPASE Y REPITA
Review and repeat

Respuestas
Answers (Cover with flap)

1 Market

1 **las alcachofas**
las alkachofas

2 **los tomates**
los tomates

3 **los guisantes**
los gheesantes

4 **los pimientos**
los peemyaintos

5 **las judías**
las hoodeeas

1 Market (3 minutes)

Name the numbered vegetables in Spanish.

1 artichokes
2 tomatoes
3 peas
4 peppers
beans 5

2 Description

1 The shoes are too expensive.
2 My room is very small.
3 I need a softer bed.

2 Description (2 minutes)

What do these sentences mean?

1 Los zapatos son demasiados caros.
2 Mi habitación es muy pequeña.
3 Necesito una cama más blanda.

3 Shops

1 **la panadería**
lah panadaireeah

2 **la joyería**
lah hoyehreeah

3 **la librería**
lah leebraireeah

4 **la pescadería**
lah peskadaireeah

5 **la pastelería**
lah pastaylaireeah

6 **la carnicería**
lah karneethaireeah

3 Shops (3 minutes)

Name the numbered shops in Spanish. Then check your answers.

1 baker

2 jeweller

3 bookshop

4 fishmonger

5 cake shop

6 butcher

4 Supermarket (3 minutes)

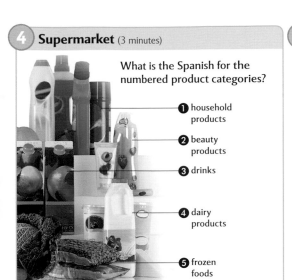

What is the Spanish for the numbered product categories?

1 household products

2 beauty products

3 drinks

4 dairy products

5 frozen foods

4 Supermarket

1 **los productos del hogar**
los pro*dook*tos del oh*gar*

2 **los productos de belleza**
los pro*dook*tos day beye*thah*

3 **las bebidas**
las be*bee*das

4 **los productos lácteos**
los pro*dook*tos *lak*teh-os

5 **la verdura**
lah ber*doo*rah

5 Museum (4 minutes)

Follow this conversation, replying in Spanish following the English prompts.

Buenos días. ¿Qué desean?
1 I'd like five tickets.

Son setenta y cinco euros.
2 That's very expensive!

No hacemos descuentos a los niños.
3 How much is a guide?

Quince euros.
4 Good. And five tickets, please.

Noventa euros, por favor.
5 Here you are. Where are the toilets?

A la derecha.
6 Thank you very much.

5 Museum

1 **Quisiera cinco entradas.**
kee*syai*rah *theen*koh en*tra*das

2 **¡Es muy caro!**
es mwee *karo*h

3 **¿Cuánto cuesta una guía?**
*kwan*toh *kwes*tah *oo*nah *ghee*ah

4 **Bien. Y cinco entradas, por favor.**
Byen. ee *theen*koh en*tra*das, por *fa*bor

5 **Aquí tiene. ¿Dónde están los servicios?**
ah*kee tye*nay. *don*day es*tan* los ser*bee*thyos

6 **Muchas gracias.**
*moo*chas *gra*thyas

1 Warm up (1 minute)

Say "from which platform?" (pp.38-9)

What is the Spanish for the following family members: sister, brother, mother, father, son, and daughter? (pp.10-11)

LAS OCUPACIONES
Jobs

Some occupations have commonly used feminine alternatives - for example, **enfermero** (*male nurse*) and **enfermera** (*female nurse*). Others remain the same. When you describe your occupation, you don't use **un/una** (*a*), saying simply **soy abogado** (*I'm a lawyer*), for example.

2 Words to remember: jobs (7 minutes)

Familiarize yourself with these words and test yourself using the cover flap. The feminine alternative is also shown.

médico *medeekoh*	doctor
dentista *denteestah*	dentist
enfermero/-a *enfermairoh/-ah*	nurse
profesor/-sora *profaysor/-sorah*	teacher
abogado/-a *abogadoh/-ah*	lawyer
contable *kontablay*	accountant
diseñador/-dora *deesenyador/-dorah*	designer
consultor/-a *konsooltor/-ah*	consultant
secretario/-a *sekraytareeoh(-ah)*	secretary
comerciante *komerthyantay*	shopkeeper
electricista *elektreetheestah*	electrician
fontanero/-a *fontanairoh/-ah*	plumber
cocinero/-a *kotheenairoh/-ah*	cook/chef
albañil *albanyeel*	builder
autónomo/-a *aootohnomoh/-ah*	self-employed

Soy fontanero.
soy fontanairoh
I'm a plumber.

Es estudiante.
es estoodyantay
She is a student.

3 Put into practice (4 minutes)

Join in this conversation. Read the Spanish on the left and follow the instructions to form your reply. Then test yourself.

¿Cuál es su profesión?
kwal es soo profesyon

What do you do?

Say: I am a consultant.

Soy consultor.
soy konsooltor

¿Para qué empresa trabaja?
parah kay empresah trabahah

What company do you work for?

Say: I'm self-employed.

Soy autónomo.
soy aootohnomoh

¡Qué interesante!
kay intairaysantay

How interesting!

Say: And what is your profession?

¿Y cuál es su profesión?
ee kwal es soo profesyon

Soy dentista.
soy denteestah

I'm a dentist.

Say: My sister is a dentist too.

Mi hermana es dentista también.
mee airrmanah es denteestah tambyen

4 Words to remember: workplace (3 minutes)

La oficina central está en Madrid.
lah ofeetheenah thentral estah en madreed
Head office is in Madrid.

Familiarize yourself with these words and test yourself.

branch	**la sucursal** *lah sookoorsal*
department	**el departamento** *el departamaintoh*
manager	**el jefe** *el hefay*
employee	**el empleado** *el emplay-ahdoh*
reception	**la recepción** *lah rrethepthyon*
trainee	**el aprendiz** *el ahprendeeth*

LA OFICINA
The office

1 Warm up (1 minute)

Practise different ways of introducing yourself in different situations (pp.8-9). Mention your name, occupation (pp. 78-9), and any other information you'd like to volunteer.

An office environment or business situation has its own vocabulary in any language, but there are many items that are virtually universal. Be aware that Spanish computer keyboards have a different layout to the standard English QWERTY convention; they also include **ñ**, vowels with accents, **¡**, and **¿**.

2 Words to remember (5 minutes)

Familiarize yourself with these words. Read them aloud several times and try to memorize them. Conceal the Spanish with the cover flap and test yourself.

el monitor *el moneetor*	monitor
el ratón *el rraton*	mouse
el correo electrónico *el korrayoh elektroneekoh*	email
el internet *el eenternet*	internet
la contraseña *lah kontrasenyah*	password
la mensajería de voz *lah mensahereeah day both*	voicemail
la contraseña de la wifi *lah kontrasenyah day lah weefee*	Wi-Fi code
la fotocopiadora *lah fotokopyadorah*	photocopier
la agenda *lah ah-hendah*	diary
la tarjeta de visita *lah tarhetah day beeseetah*	business card
la reunión *lah reh-oonyon*	meeting
la conferencia *lah konfairentheeah*	conference
el orden del día *el orden del deeah*	agenda

lamp ❶

screen ❹

laptop ❻

keyboard ❹

❷ stapler

telephone ❸

drawer ❿

pen ❿　❶ notepad

❼ desk

3 Useful phrases (2 minutes)

Learn these phrases and then test yourself using the cover flap.

I need to make some photocopies.	**Necesito hacer unas fotocopias.** *netheseetoh ahther oonas fotokopyas*
I'd like to arrange an appointment.	**Quisiera organizar una cita.** *keesyairah organeethar oonah theetah*
I want to send an email.	**Quiero mandar un correo electrónico.** *kyairoh mandar oon korrayoh elektroneekoh*

4 Match and repeat (5 minutes)

Match the numbered items to the Spanish words on the left.

clock **8**

printer **9**

13 swivel chair

5 Say it (2 minutes)

I'd like to arrange a conference.

I have a laptop.

Do you have email?

1 la lámpara
lah lamparah

2 la grapadora
lah grapadohrah

3 el teléfono
el telefonoh

4 la pantalla
lah pantayah

5 el teclado
el tekladoh

6 el portátil
el portateel

7 la mesa de escritorio
lah mesah day eskreetoryoh

8 el reloj
el rrelokh

9 la impresora
lah impresorah

10 el bolígrafo
el boleegrafoh

11 el bloc
el blok

12 el cajón
el kahon

13 la silla giratoria
lah seeyah heeratoreeah

EL MUNDO ACADÉMICO
Academic world

In Spain, students are selected for a first degree (**una licenciatura**) by an average of secondary school grades and an exam. After graduation, some students go on to **un máster** (master's degree) or **un doctora do** (PhD).

2 Useful phrases (3 minutes)

Practise these phrases and then test yourself using the cover flap.

¿Cuál es su especialidad? *kwal es soo espetheeahleedad*	What is your field?
Hago investigación en bioquímica. *ahgoh inbesteegathyon en beeohkeemeekah*	I am doing research in biochemistry.
Soy licenciado en derecho. *soy leethentheeahdoh en derechoh*	I have a degree in law.
Voy a dar una conferencia sobre arquitectura. *boy ah dar oonah kon-fairayntheeah sobreh arkeetektoorah*	I'm going to give a lecture on architecture.

3 In conversation (5 minutes)

Hola, soy la profesora Fernández.
o-lah, soy lah profaysorah fernandeth

Hello, I'm Professor Fernandez.

¿De qué universidad es usted?
deh keh ooneeberseedad es oosted

What university are you from?

De la Universidad de Murcia.
deh lah ooneeberseedad deh moortheeah

From the University of Murcia.

4 Words to remember (4 minutes)

Familiarize yourself with these words and then test yourself.

Tenemos un stand en la feria.
tenemos oon estand en la fereeah
We have a stand at the trade fair.

conference/lecture	**la conferencia** *lah konfairraintheeah*
trade fair	**la feria** *lah fereeah*
seminar	**el seminario** *el semeenaryoh*
lecture theatre	**el anfiteatro** *el anfeetay-ahtroh*
conference room	**la sala de conferencias** *lah sahlah deh konferaintheeas*
exhibition	**la exposición** *lah eksposeethyon*
library	**la biblioteca** *lah bibleeotekah*
university lecturer	**el profesor de universidad** *el profaysor deh ooneeberseedad*
professor	**el catedrático** *el katedrateekoh*
medicine	**medicina** *medeetheenah*
science	**ciencias** *thyaintheeas*
literature	**literatura** *leetairatoorah*
engineering	**ingeniería** *inhainyaireeah*

5 Say it (2 minutes)

I'm doing research in medicine.

I have a degree in literature.

She's the professor.

¿Cuál es su especialidad?
kwal es soo espethyaleedad

What's your field?

Hago investigación en ingeniería.
ahgoh inbesteegathyon en inhenyaireeah

I'm doing research in engineering.

¡Qué interesante! Yo también.
keh intairaysantay. yoh tambeeayn

How interesting! Me too.

LOS NEGOCIOS
In business

You will receive a more friendly reception and make a good impression if you make the effort to begin a meeting with a short introduction in Spanish, even if your vocabulary is limited. After that, all parties will probably be happy to continue the proceedings in English.

2 Words to remember (6 minutes)

Familiarize yourself with these words and then test yourself by concealing the Spanish with the cover flap.

el cliente
el klyaintay
client

el informe
el informay
report

el programa *el programah*	schedule
la entrega *lah entraygah*	delivery
el pago *el pahgoh*	payment
el presupuesto *el praysoopwestoh*	budget/ estimate
el precio *el praythyoh*	price
el documento *el dokoomentoh*	document
la factura *lah faktoorah*	invoice
la propuesta *lah propwestah*	proposal
los beneficios *los baynayfeethyos*	profits
las ventas *las bentas*	sales
los números *los noomeros*	figures

Cultural tip A long lunch with wine is still a regular feature of doing business in Spain. As a visiting client you can expect to be taken out to a restaurant, and as a supplier you should consider entertaining your business customers.

3 Useful phrases (6 minutes)

Practise these useful business phrases and then test yourself using the cover flap.

Me manda el contrato, por favor.
may mandah el kontratoh, por fabor

Please send me the contract.

¿Firmamos el contrato?
feermamos el kontratoh
Shall we sign the contract?

el ejecutivo
el eh-hekooteeboh
executive

¿Hemos acordado un programa?
ehmos akordadoh oon programah

Have we agreed a schedule?

el contrato
el kontratoh
contract

¿Cuándo puede hacer la entrega?
kwandoh pweday ahther lah entregah

When can you make the delivery?

¿Cuál es el presupuesto?
kwal es el praysoopwestoh

What's the budget?

4 Say it (2 minutes)

Can you send me the estimate?

Have we agreed a price?

What are the profits?

¿Me puede mandar la factura?
may pweday mandar lah faktoorah

Can you send me the invoice?

REPASE Y REPITA
Review and repeat

Respuestas
Answers (Cover with flap)

1 At the office

1 la grapadora
lah grapadorah

2 la lámpara
lah lamparah

3 el portátil
el portateel

4 el bolígrafo
el boleegrafoh

5 el reloj
el rrelokh

6 el bloc
el blok

7 la mesa de escritorio
lah mesah day eskreetoryoh

1 At the office (4 minutes)

Name these items.

lamp **2** · **3** laptop · pen **4** · clock **5** · stapler **1** · **7** desk · **6** notepad

2 Jobs

1 médico
medeekoh

2 fontanero/-a
fontanairoh/-ah

3 comerciante
komerthyantay

4 contable
kontablay

5 estudiante
estoodyantay

6 abogado/-a
abogadoh/-ah

2 Jobs (3 minutes)

What are these jobs in Spanish?

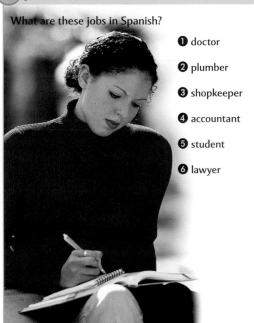

1 doctor
2 plumber
3 shopkeeper
4 accountant
5 student
6 lawyer

3 Work (4 minutes)

Answer these questions following the English prompts.

¿Para qué empresa trabaja?
❶ Say: I am self-employed.

¿En qué universidad está?
❷ Say: I'm at the University of Salamanca.

¿Cuál es su especialidad?
❸ Say: I'm doing research in medicine.

¿Hemos acordado un programa?
❹ Say: Yes, my secretary has the schedule.

3 Work

❶ **Soy autónomo.**
soy aootonomoh

❷ **Estoy en la Universidad de Salamanca.**
estoy en lah ooneeberseedad day salamankah

❸ **Hago investigación en medicina.**
ahgoh inbesteegathyon en medeetheenah

❹ **Sí. mi secretaria tiene el programa.**
see. mee sekretareeah tyenay el programah

4 How much? (4 minutes)

Answer the question with the amount shown in brackets.

❶ **¿Cuánto cuesta el desayuno?** (€3.50)

❷ **¿Cuánto cuesta la habitación?** (€47)

❸ **¿Cuánto cuesta un kilo de tomates?** (€3.25)

❹ **¿Cuánto cuesta un plaza para cuatro noches?** (€60)

4 How much?

❶ **Son tres euros cincuenta.**
son tres eh-ooros theenkwentah

❷ **Son cuarenta y siete euros.**
son kwarentah ee seeaytay eh-ooros

❸ **Son tres euros veinticinco.**
son tres eh-ooros beynteetheenkoh

❹ **Son sesenta euros.**
son sesentah eh-ooros

1 Warm up (1 minute)

Say "I'm allergic to nuts". (pp.24-5)

Say the verb "tener" (to have) in all its forms: yo, tú, él/ella, nosotros(-as), vosotros(-as), ellos (-as). (pp.14-15)

EN LA FARMACIA
At the chemist

Spanish pharmacists are qualified to give advice and sell over-the-counter medicines, as well as dispense prescription medicines. There is generally a **farmacia de guardia** (*duty pharmacy*) to provide 24-hour service in every town – a list is displayed in every pharmacy.

2 Match and repeat (3 minutes)

Match the numbered items to the Spanish words in the panel on the left and test yourself using the cover flap.

❶ **la venda**
   lah bendah

❷ **el jarabe**
   el harabay

❸ **las gotas**
   las gotas

❹ **la tirita**
   lah teereetah

❺ **la jeringuilla**
   lah hereengheeyah

❻ **la crema**
   lah kremah

❼ **el supositorio**
   el sooposeetoryoh

❽ **la pastilla**
   lah pasteeyah

syrup ❷

bandage ❶

❻ cream

drops ❸

plaster ❹

syringe ❺

3 In conversation (3 minutes)

Buenos días, señor. ¿Qué desea?
bwenos deeyas, senyor. kay desayah

Good morning, sir. What would you like?

Tengo dolor de estómago.
tengoh dolor day estomagoh

I have a stomach ache.

¿Tiene diarrea?
tyenay deeahrrayah

Do you have diarrhoea?

4 Words to remember (2 minutes)

Familiarize yourself with these words and test yourself using the cover flap.

Tengo dolor de cabeza.
tengoh dolor day kabethah

I have a headache.

headache	**el dolor de cabeza** *el dolor day kabethah*
stomach ache	**el dolor de estómago** *el dolor day estomagoh*
diarrhoea	**la diarrea** *lah deeahrrayah*
cold	**el resfriado** *el rresfreeahdoh*
cough	**la tos** *lah tos*
sunstroke	**la insolación** *lah eensolatheeyon*
toothache	**el dolor de muelas** *el dolor day mwelas*

6 Say it (2 minutes)

I have a cold.

Do you have that as a cream?

He has toothache.

7 suppository

8 tablet

5 Useful phrases (4 minutes)

Practise these phrases and then test yourself using the cover flap.

I have sunstroke.	**Tengo una insolación.** *tengoh oonah eensolatheeyon*
Do you have that as a syrup?	**¿Lo tiene en jarabe?** *loh tyenay en harabay*
I'm allergic to penicillin.	**Soy alérgico a la penicilina.** *soy alerheekoh ah lah peneetheeleenah*

No, pero tengo dolor de cabeza.
noh, peroh tengoh dolor day kabethah

No, but I have a headache.

Aquí tiene.
ahkee tyenay

Here you are.

¿Lo tiene en pastilla?
loh tyenay en pasteeyah

Do you have this as pills?

EL CUERPO
The body

You are most likely to need to refer to parts of the body in the context of illness - for example, when describing aches and pains to a doctor. The most common phrases for talking about discomfort are **Tengo un dolor en la/el...** (*I have a pain in the...*) and **Me duele la/el...** (*My ... hurts me*).

1 Warm up (1 minute)

Say "I have a toothache" and "I have a sunstroke". (pp.88-9)

Say the Spanish for "red", "green", "black", and "yellow". (pp.74-5)

2 Match and repeat: body (6 minutes)

Match the numbered parts of the body with the list on the left. Test yourself by using the cover flap.

❶ **la mano**
   lah manoh

❷ **la cabeza**
   lah kabethah

❸ **el hombro**
   el ombroh

❹ **el codo**
   el kodoh

❺ **el pelo**
   el peloh

❻ **el brazo**
   el brathoh

❼ **el cuello**
   el kweyoh

❽ **el pecho**
   el pechoh

❾ **el estómago**
   el estomagoh

❿ **la pierna**
   lah pyairnah

⓫ **la rodilla**
   lah rrodeeyah

⓬ **el pie**
   el pee-ay

❶ hand
❹ elbow
❺ hair
❷ head
❻ arm
shoulder ❸
❼ neck
chest ❽
stomach ❾
leg ❿
knee ⓫
⓬ foot

3 Match and repeat: face (3 minutes)

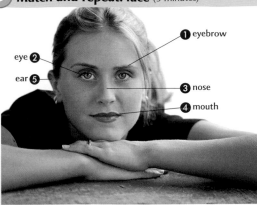

- ❶ eyebrow
- eye ❷
- ear ❺
- ❸ nose
- ❹ mouth

Match the numbered facial features with the list on the right.

❶ **la ceja**
lah thayah

❷ **el ojo**
el oh-hoh

❸ **la nariz**
lah nareeth

❹ **la boca**
lah bokah

❺ **la oreja**
lah ohrayah

4 Useful phrases (3 minutes)

Learn these phrases and then test yourself using the cover flap.

I have a pain in my back.	**Tengo un dolor en la espalda.** *tengoh oon dolor en lah espalda*
I have a rash on my arm.	**Tengo un sarpullido en el brazo.** *tengoh oon sarpooyeedoh en el brathoh*
I don't feel well.	**No me encuentro bien.** *noh may enkwentroh byen*

5 Put into practice (2 minutes)

Join in this conversation and test yourself using the cover flap.

¿Cuál es el problema?
kwal es el problemah

What's the problem?

Say: I don't feel well.

No me encuentro bien.
noh may enkwentroh byen

¿Dónde le duele?
donday lay dwelay

Where does it hurt?

Say: I have a pain in the shoulder.

Tengo un dolor en el hombro.
tengoh oon dolor en el ombroh

EN EL MÉDICO
At the doctor

Unless it's an emergency, you have to book an appointment with the doctor and pay when you leave. You can usually reclaim the money if you have medical insurance. Your hotel, a local pharmacy, or a tourist information office may be able to tell you the names and addresses of local doctors.

1 Warm up (1 minute)

Say "I need some tablets". (pp.60-1, pp.88-9)

Say "He needs some cream". (pp.88-9)

What is the Spanish for "I don't have a son". (pp.10-15)

2 Useful phrases you may hear (3 minutes)

Practise these phrases and then test yourself using the cover flap to conceal the Spanish on the left.

No es grave. *noh es gravay*	It's not serious.
Necesita hacerse unas pruebas. *netheseetah ahthersay oonas prwaybas*	You need to have some tests.
Tiene una infección de riñón. *tyenay oonah infekthyon day rreenyon*	You have a kidney infection.
Necesita ir al hospital. *netheseetah eer al ospeetal*	You need to go to hospital.

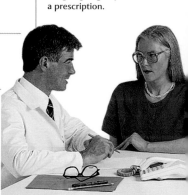

Le voy a dar una receta.
lay boy ah dar oonah rrethetah
I'm going to give you a prescription.

3 In conversation (5 minutes)

¿Cuál es el problema?
kwal es el problemah

What's the problem?

Tengo un dolor en el pecho.
tengoh oon dolor en el pechoh

I have a pain in my chest.

Déjeme que la examine.
dayhaymay kay lah eksameenay

Let me examine you.

4 Useful phrases you may need to say (4 minutes)

Estoy embarazada.
es<u>*toy*</u> *embara*<u>*tha*</u>*dah*
I am pregnant.

Practise these phrases and then test yourself using the cover flap.

I am diabetic.	**Soy diabético/-a.** *soy deeah*<u>*bete*</u>*ekoh/-ah*
I am epileptic.	**Soy epiléptico/-a.** *soy epee*<u>*lep*</u>*teekoh/-ah*
I'm asthmatic.	**Soy asmático/-a.** *soy as*<u>*ma*</u>*teekoh/-ah*
I have a heart condition.	**Tengo un problema de corazón.** <u>*teng*</u>*oh oon pro*<u>*blem*</u>*ah day korathon*
I have a temperature.	**Tengo fiebre.** <u>*teng*</u>*oh* <u>*fyay*</u>*bray*
I feel faint.	**Estoy mareado.** *es*<u>*toy*</u> *maray-*<u>*ah*</u>*doh*
It's urgent.	**Es urgente.** *es oor*<u>*hen*</u>*tay*

Conversational tip

If you are an EU national, you are entitled to free emergency medical treatment in Spain on production of a European Health Insurance Card or an E111 form. For an ambulance, call 112.

5 Say it (2 minutes)

My son is diabetic.

I have a pain in my arm.

It's not urgent.

¿Es grave?
es <u>*gra*</u>*vay*

Is it serious?

No, sólo tiene indigestión.
noh, <u>*soloh*</u> <u>*tye*</u>*nay indeehestyon*

No, you only have indigestion.

¡Menos mal!
<u>*may*</u>*nos mal*

What a relief!

1 Warm up (1 minute)

Say "How long is the journey?" (pp.42-3)

Ask "Is is serious?" (pp.92-3)

What is the Spanish for "mouth" and "head"? (pp.90-1)

EN EL HOSPITAL
At the hospital

It is useful to know a few basic phrases relating to hospitals and medical treatment for use in an emergency, or in case you need to visit a friend or colleague in hospital. Most Spanish hospitals have only two beds per room and their own en-suite bathroom facilities.

2 Useful phrases (5 minutes)

Familiarize yourself with these phrases. Conceal the Spanish with the cover flap and test yourself.

¿Cuáles son las horas de visita? _kwales son las oras day beeseetah_	What are the visiting hours?
¿Cuánto tiempo va a tardar? _kwantoh tyempoh bah ah tardar_	How long will it take?
¿Va a doler? _bah ah doler_	Will it hurt?
Túmbese aquí por favor. _toombesay ahkee por fabor_	Please lie down here.
No puede comer nada. _noh pweday komer nadah_	You cannot eat anything.
No mueva la cabeza. _noh mwebah lah kabethah_	Don't move your head.
Abra la boca por favor. _ahbrah lah bokah por fabor_	Please open your mouth.
Necesita un análisis de sangre. _netheseetah oon analeesees day sangray_	You need a blood test.

¿Se encuentra mejor? _say enkwentrah mehor_ Are you feeling better?

¿Dónde está la sala de espera? _donday estah lah salah day esperah_ Where is the waiting room?

el gotero _el goteroh_ drip

3 Words to remember (4 minutes)

Familiarize yourself with these words and test yourself using the cover flap.

emergency department	**el servicio de urgencias** *el serbeethyoh day oorhentheeas*
x-ray department	**el servicio de radiología** *el serbeethyoh day rradyoloheeah*
children's ward	**la sala de pediatría** *lah salah day pedeeatreeah*
operating theatre	**el quirófano** *el keerofanoh*
waiting room	**la sala de espera** *lah salah day esperah*
stairs	**las escaleras** *las eskaleras*

Su radiografía es normal.
soo rradyografeeah es normal
Your x-ray is normal.

4 Put into practice (3 minutes)

Join in this conversation. Cover up the text on the right and complete the anwering part of the dialogue in Spanish. Check your answers and repeat if necessary.

Tiene una infección. *tyenay oonah infekthyon*

You have an infection.

Ask: Do I need tests?

¿Necesito hacerme pruebas? *netheseetoh ahthermay prwaybas*

Primero necesita un análisis de sangre. *preemeroh netheseetah oon analeesees day sangray*

First you will need a blood test.

Ask: Will it hurt?

¿Me va a doler? *may bah ah doler*

5 Say it (2 minutes)

Does he need a blood test?

Where is the children's ward?

Do I need an x-ray?

No, no se preocupe. *noh, noh say pray-okoopay*

No. Don't worry.

Ask: How long will it take?

¿Cuánto tiempo va a tardar? *kwantoh tyempoh bah ah tardar*

REPASE Y REPITA
Review and repeat

1 The body

❶ **la cabeza**
lah kabethah

❷ **el brazo**
el brathoh

❸ **el pecho**
el pechoh

❹ **el estómago**
el estomagoh

❺ **la pierna**
lah pyairnah

❻ **la rodilla**
lah rrodeeyah

❼ **el pie**
el pee-ay

1 The body (4 minutes)

Name the numbered
body parts in Spanish.

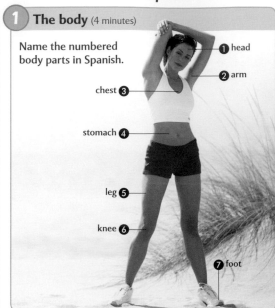

❶ head
❷ arm
chest ❸
stomach ❹
leg ❺
knee ❻
❼ foot

2 On the phone

❶ **Quisiera hablar con Ana Flores.**
keesyairah hablar kon anna flores

❷ **Luis Cortés de Don Frío.**
looees kortes day don free-oh

❸ **¿Puedo dejar un mensaje?**
pwedoh dehar oon mensahay

❹ **La cita el lunes a las once está bien.**
lah theetah el loones ah las onthay estah byen

❺ **Gracias, adiós.**
grathyas, addy-os

2 On the phone (4 minutes)

You are arranging an appointment. Follow the
conversation, replying in Spanish following
the English prompts.

Dígame, Apex Finanzas.
❶ I'd like to speak to Ana Flores.

¿De parte de quién?
❷ Luis Cortés, of Don Frío.

Lo siento, está comunicando.
❸ Can I leave a message?

Sí, dígame.
❹ The appointment on Monday at 11am is fine.

Muy bien, adiós.
❺ Thank you, goodbye.

3 Clothing (3 minutes)

Say the Spanish words for the numbered items of clothing.

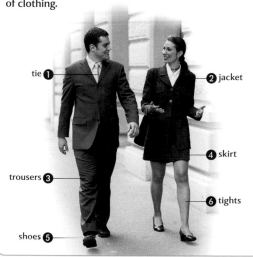

tie ❶

❷ jacket

❹ skirt

trousers ❸

❻ tights

shoes ❺

3 Clothing

❶ **la corbata**
lah korbatah

❷ **la chaqueta**
lah chaketah

❸ **el pantalón**
el pantalon

❹ **la falda**
lah faldah

❺ **los zapatos**
los thapatos

❻ **las medias**
las medeeas

4 At the doctor's (4 minutes)

Say these phrases in Spanish.

❶ I don't feel well.
❷ I have a heart condition.
❸ Do I need to go to hospital?
❹ I am pregnant.

4 At the doctor's

❶ **No me encuentro bien.**
noh may enkwentroh byen

❷ **Tengo un problema de corazón.**
tengoh oon problemah day korathon

❸ **¿Necesito ir al hospital?**
netheseetoh eer al ospeetal

❹ **Estoy embarazada.**
estoy embarathadah

1 Warm up (1 minute)

Say the months of
the year in Spanish.
(pp.28–9)

Ask "Is there a car park?"
and "Are there toilets?"
(pp.48–9 and pp.62–3)

EN CASA
At home

Many city-dwellers live in apartment blocks
(**edificios**), but in rural areas the houses tend to
be detached (**chalet**). If you want to know how
big it is you will need to ask in square metres.
If you want to know how many bedrooms
there are ask **¿Cuántos dormitorios hay?**.

2 Match and repeat (5 minutes)

Match the numbered items to the list and test
yourself using the flap.

❶ **la chimenea**
   lah cheeme<u>nay</u>ah

❷ **la ventana**
   lah ben<u>tan</u>ah

❸ **el tejado**
   el te<u>had</u>oh

❹ **la terraza**
   lah te<u>rra</u>tha

❺ **la persiana**
   lah persee<u>an</u>ah

❻ **el muro**
   el <u>moor</u>oh

❼ **la puerta**
   lah <u>pwer</u>tah

❽ **el garaje**
   el <u>gar</u>ahay

chimney ❶   ❷ window   roof ❸

shutters ❺

door ❼

wall ❻

Cultural tip You almost never see a Spanish home without
shutters at every window. These are closed at night and often
during the heat of the day in summer. Curtains, where they exist
at all, tend to be more for decoration. Carpets are not popular in
Spanish homes; ceramic tiles or parquet floors with rugs are a
more common flooring solution.

3 Words to remember (4 minutes)

¿Cuánto es el alquiler al mes?
kwantoh es el alkeeler al mes
What is the rent per month?

Familiarize yourself with these words and test yourself using the cover flap.

room	**la habitación** *lah abeetathyon*
floor	**el suelo** *el sweloh*
ceiling	**el techo** *el techoh*
bedroom	**el dormitorio** *el dormeetoreeoh*
bathroom	**el cuarto de baño** *el kwartoh day banyoh*
kitchen	**la cocina** *lah kotheenah*
dining room	**el comedor** *el komedor*
living room	**el cuarto de estar** *el kwartoh day estar*
cellar	**el sótano** *el sotahnoh*
attic	**el ático** *el ahteekoh*

terrace ④

garage ⑧

4 Useful phrases (3 minutes)

Practise these phrases and test yourself.

¿Hay un garaje?
ah-ee oon garahay

Is there a garage?

¿Cuándo está disponible?
kwandoh estah deesponeeblay

When is it available?

¿Está amueblado?
estah amwebladoh

Is it furnished?

5 Say it (2 minutes)

Is there a dining room?

Is it large?

Is it available in July?

EN LA CASA
Inside the house

If you're renting a holiday house or villa in Spain, the most usual option is to take it for a full month or, if not, for a **quincena**, the first or last fifteen days of the month. You will need to check in advance whether the cost of utilities is included in the rent. Most holiday homes have no telephone.

2 **Match and repeat** (3 minutes)

Match the numbered items to the list in the panel on the left. Then test yourself by concealing the Spanish with the cover flap.

❶ **la encimera**
lah entheemerah

❷ **el fregadero**
el fregaderoh

❸ **el microondas**
el meekro-ondas

❹ **el horno**
el ornoh

❺ **la cocina**
lah kotheenah

❻ **el frigorífico**
el freegoreefeekoh

❼ **la mesa**
lah mesah

❽ **la silla**
lah seeyah

❺ cooker ❶ worktop
❻ fridge
chair ❽
❹ oven   table ❼

3 **In conversation** (3 minutes)

Este es el horno.
estay es el ornoh

This is the oven.

¿Hay también un lavavajillas?
ah-ee tambyen oon lababaheeyas

Is there a dishwasher as well?

Sí, y hay un congelador grande.
see, ee ah-ee oon konhelador granday

Yes, and there's a big freezer.

4 Words to remember (2 minutes)

Familiarize yourself with these words and test yourself using the cover flap.

El sofá es nuevo.
el sofah es nweboh
The sofa is new.

wardrobe	**el armario** *el armaryoh*	
sofa	**el sofá** *el sofah*	
fireplace	**la chimenea** *lah cheemenayah*	
carpet	**la moqueta** *lah moketah*	
bath	**la bañera** *lah banyerah*	
toilet	**el váter** *el bater*	
wash basin	**el lavabo** *el lababoh*	

❷ sink   microwave ❸

5 Useful phrases (4 minutes)

Practise these phrases and then test yourself.

The cooker is broken.	**La cocina no funciona.** *lah kotheenah noh foonthyonah*
I don't like the curtains.	**No me gustan las cortinas.** *noh may goostan las korteenas*
Is electricity included?	**¿Está incluida la electricidad?** *estah eenklooeedah lah ehektreetheedad*

6 Say it (2 minutes)

Is there a microwave?

I like the fireplace.

What a soft sofa!

Todo está muy nuevo. *todoh estah mwee nweboh*

Everything is very new.

Y aquí está la lavadora. *ee ahkee estah lah labadorah*

And here's the washing machine.

¡Qué azulejos más bonitos! *kay ah-thoolayhos mas boneetos*

What beautiful tiles!

EL JARDÍN
The garden

The garden of a house or a villa may be communal, or at least partly shared. Check with the estate agent or rental agent carefully to establish the position. In some cases, a charge for upkeep of the garden may be included with the rent of an apartment. Check with the agent.

2 Words to remember (3 minutes)

Familiarize yourself with these words and test yourself using the cover flap.

la máquina cortacésped *lah makeenah kortathesped*	lawn mower
la horca *lah orkah*	fork
la pala *lah palah*	spade
el rastrillo *el rrastreeyoh*	rake
el vivero *el beeberoh*	garden centre

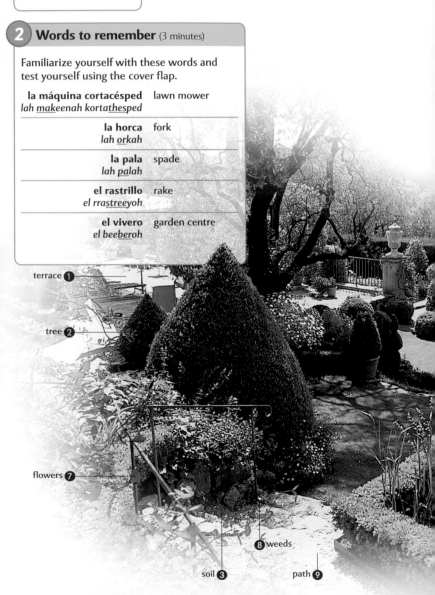

terrace ❶

tree ❷

flowers ❼

❽ weeds

soil ❸

path ❾

3 Useful phrases (4 minutes)

Practise these phrases and then test yourself using the cover flap.

The gardener comes once a week.	**El jardinero viene una vez a la semana.** *el hardee__nairoh__ byai__nay__ __oo__nah beth ah lah se__manah__*
Can you mow the lawn?	**¿Puede cortar el césped?** *__pwe__day kor__tar__ el __thes__ped*
Is the garden private?	**¿Es el jardín privado?** *es el har__deen__ pree__ba__doh*
The garden needs watering.	**El jardín necesita que lo rieguen.** *el har__deen__ nethe__seetah__ kay loh __rreeayghen__*

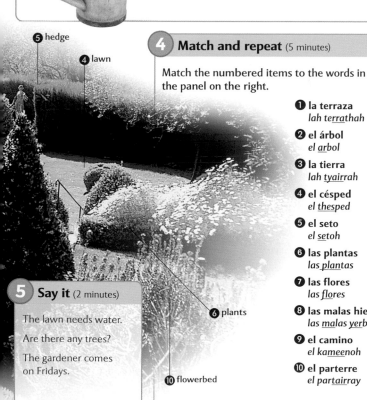

❺ hedge

❹ lawn

❻ plants

❿ flowerbed

4 Match and repeat (5 minutes)

Match the numbered items to the words in the panel on the right.

❶ **la terraza**
  lah te__rra__thah

❷ **el árbol**
  el __ar__bol

❸ **la tierra**
  lah __tyai__rrah

❹ **el césped**
  el __thes__ped

❺ **el seto**
  el __se__toh

❻ **las plantas**
  las __plan__tas

❼ **las flores**
  las __flo__res

❽ **las malas hierbas**
  las __malas yer__bas

❾ **el camino**
  el ka__mee__noh

❿ **el parterre**
  el par__tair__ray

5 Say it (2 minutes)

The lawn needs water.

Are there any trees?

The gardener comes on Fridays.

LOS ANIMALES DE COMPAÑÍA
Pets

1 Warm up (1 minute)

Say "My name's ...".
(pp.8-9)

Say "Don't worry".
(pp.94-5)

What's "your" in Spanish?
(pp.12-13)

"Pet passports" are now available to enable holiday-makers and commuters to take their pets with them to Spain and avoid quarantine on return to the UK. Consult your vet for details on the necessary vaccinations and paperwork.

2 Match and repeat (3 minutes)

Match the numbered animals to the Spanish words in the panel on the left. Then test yourself using the cover flap.

❶ **el gato**
el gatoh

❷ **el conejo**
el konehoh

❸ **el pájaro**
el paharoh

❹ **el pez**
el peth

❺ **el perro**
el perroh

❻ **el hámster**
el hamster

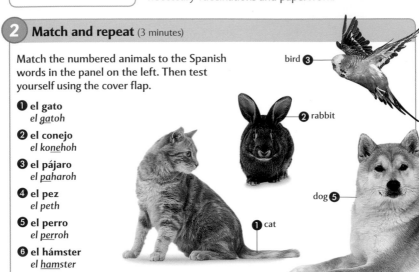

bird ❸
❷ rabbit
dog ❺
❶ cat

3 Useful phrases (4 minutes)

Learn these phrases and then test yourself using the cover flap.

¿Es bueno el perro? *es bwenoh el perroh*	Is this dog friendly?
¿Puedo llevar el perro? *pwedoh yebar el perroh*	Can I bring my dog?
Me dan miedo los gatos. *may dan myaydoh los gatos*	I'm frightened of cats.
Mi perro no muerde. *mee perroh noh mweday*	My dog doesn't bite.

Este gato está lleno de pulgas.
estay gatoh estah yenoh day poolgas
This cat is full of fleas.

Cultural tip Many dogs in Spain are working or guard dogs and you may encounter them tethered or roaming free. Approach farms and rural houses with particular care. Look out for warning notices such as **¡Cuidado con el perro!** (*Beware of the dog*).

¡CUIDADO CON EL PERRO!

Mi perro no está bien.
mee perroh noh estah byen
My dog is not well.

⑥ hamster

fish ④

4 Words to remember (4 minutes)

Familiarize yourself with these words and test yourself using the cover flap.

basket	**la cesta**
	lah thestah
cage	**la jaula**
	lah haoolah
bowl	**el bol**
	el bol
collar	**el collar**
	el koyar
lead	**la correa**
	lah korray-ah
vet	**el veterinario**
	el betereenaryoh
vaccination	**la vacuna**
	lah bakoonah
pet passport	**el pasaporte de animales**
	el pasaportay day aneemales
flea spray	**el spray antipulgas**
	el espraee anteepoolgas

5 Put into practice (3 minutes)

Join in this conversation. Read the Spanish on the left and follow the instructions to make your reply. Then test yourself by concealing the answers with the cover flap.

¿Es suyo este perro?
es sooyoh estay perroh
Is this your dog?

Say: Yes, he's called Sandy.

Sí, se llama Sandy.
see, say yamah Sandy

Me dan miedo los perros.
may dan myaydoh los perros
I'm frightened of dogs.

Say: Don't worry. He's friendly.

No se preocupe. Es bueno.
noh say prayohkoopay. es bwenoh

Respuestas
Answers (Cover with flap)

REPASE Y REPITA
Review and repeat

1 Colours

❶ negra
negrah

❷ pequeños
pekenyos

❸ rojo
rrohoh

❹ verde
berday

❺ amarillos
amareeyos

1 Colours (4 minutes)

Complete the sentences with the Spanish word
for the colour in brackets. Watch out for masculine
and feminine.

❶ Quisiera la camisa _____. (black)

❷ Estos zapatos son muy _____. (small)

❸ ¿Tiene este traje en _____? (red)

❹ No, pero lo tengo en _____. (green)

❺ Quiero los zapatos _____. (yellow)

2 Kitchen

❶ la cocina
lah kotheenah

❷ el frigorífico
el freegoreefeekoh

❸ el fregadero
el fregaderoh

❹ el microondas
el meekro-ondas

❺ el horno
el ornoh

❻ la silla
lah seeyah

❼ la mesa
lah mesah

2 Kitchen (4 minutes)

Say the Spanish words for the numbered items.

cooker ❶   fridge ❷

❺ oven   chair ❻

3 House (4 minutes)

You are visiting a house in Spain. Join in the conversation, asking questions in Spanish following the English prompts.

Éste es el cuarto de estar.
❶ What a lovely fireplace.

Sí, y tiene una cocina muy grande.
❷ How many bedrooms are there?

Hay tres dormitorios.
❸ Do you have a garage?

Sí, pero no hay un jardín.
❹ When is it available?

En julio.
❺ What is the rent a month?

3 House

❶ ¡Qué chimenea más bonita!
kay cheemenayah mas boneetah

❷ ¿Cuántos dormitorios hay?
kwantos dormeetoreeos ah-ee

❸ ¿Tiene garaje?
tyenay garahay

❹ ¿Cuándo está disponible?
kwandoh estah deesponeeblay

❺ ¿Cuánto es el alquiler al mes?
kwantoh es el alkeeler al mes

4 At home (3 minutes)

microwave ❹
❸ sink
table ❼

Say the Spanish for the following items.

❶ washing machine
❷ sofa
❸ attic
❹ dining room
❺ tree
❻ garden

4 At home

❶ la lavadora
lah labadorah

❷ el sofá
el sofah

❸ el ático
el ahteekoh

❹ el comedor
el komedor

❺ el árbol
el arbol

❻ el jardín
el hardeen

EL BANCO Y LA OFICINA DE CORREOS
Bank and post office

1 Warm up (1 minute)

Ask "How do I get to the bank?" and "How do I get to the post office?" (pp.50-1)

What's the Spanish for "passport"? (pp.54-5)

How do you ask "What time is the meeting?" (pp.30-1)

Banks and post offices usually open only until lunchtime (approximately 2pm) and are generally closed at weekends. **Cajas de ahorros** (*savings banks*) have different hours. In summer, operation times may be shorter.

2 Words to remember: post (3 minutes)

Familiarize yourself with these words and test yourself using the cover flap to conceal the Spanish on the left.

los sellos *los seyos*	stamps
la postal *lah postal*	postcard
el paquete *el paketay*	parcel
por avión *por abyon*	by air mail
el correo certificado *el korrayoh therteefeekadoh*	registered post
el buzón *el boothon*	post box
el código postal *el kodeegoh postal*	postcode
el cartero *el kartairoh*	postman

el sobre
el sobray
envelope

¿Cuánto es para el Reino Unido?
kwantoh es parah el rrayeenoh ooneedoh
How much is it for the United Kingdom?

3 In conversation (3 minutes)

Quisiera sacar dinero.
keesyairah sakar deeneroh

I'd like to withdraw some money.

¿Tiene identificación?
tyenay eedenteefeekathyon

Do you have any ID?

Sí, aquí tiene mi pasaporte.
see, ahkee tyenay mee pasaportay

Yes, here's my passport.

¿Cómo puedo pagar?
komoh pwedoh pagar
How can I pay?

4 Words to remember: bank (2 minutes)

Familiarize yourself with these words and test yourself using the cover flap to cover the Spanish on the right.

PIN	**el pin** *el peen*
bank	**el banco** *el bankoh*
cashier	**el cajero** *el kaheroh*
cashpoint/ATM	**el cajero automático** *el kaheroh aootomateekoh*
notes	**los billetes** *los beeyetes*
credit card	**la tarjeta de crédito** *lah tarhetah day kredeetoh*

5 Useful phrases (4 minutes)

Practise these phrases and then test yourself using the cover flap.

I'd like to change some money.	**Quisiera cambiar dinero.** *keesyairah kambyar deeneroh*
What is the exchange rate?	**¿A cuánto está el cambio?** *ah kwantoh estah el kambyoh*
I'd like to withdraw some money.	**Quisiera sacar dinero.** *keesyairah sakar deeneroh*

6 Say it (2 minutes)

I'd like to pay by credit card.

Do I need my PIN?

I'd like a stamp for the United Kingdom.

Meta su pin, por favor.
metah soo peen, por fabor

Please key in your PIN.

¿Tengo que firmar también?
tengoh kay feermar tambyen

Do I have to sign as well?

No, no hace falta.
noh, noh ahthay faltah

No, that's not necessary.

LOS SERVICIOS
Services

1 Warm up (1 minute)

What is the Spanish for "doesn't work"? (pp.60-1)

What's the Spanish for "today" and "tomorrow"? (pp.28-9)

You can combine the Spanish words on these pages with the vocabulary you learned in week 10 to help you explain basic problems and cope with arranging most repairs. When organizing construction work or a repair, it's a good idea to agree to the price and method of payment in advance.

2 Words to remember (4 minutes)

Familiarize yourself with these words and test yourself using the cover flap.

el fontanero *el fontanairoh*	plumber
el electricista *el ehlektreetheestah*	electrician
el mecánico *el mekaneekoh*	mechanic
el albañil *el albanyeel*	builder
la asistenta *lah aseestentah*	cleaner
el pintor *el peentor*	decorator
el carpintero *el karpeenteroh*	carpenter
el técnico *el tekneekoh*	technician

la llave de tuercas
lah yabay day twerkas
wheel brace

No necesito un mecánico.
noh netheseetoh oon mekaneekoh
I don't need a mechanic.

3 In conversation (3 minutes)

La lavadora no funciona.
lah labadorah noh foothyonah

The washing machine's not working.

Sí, la manguera está rota.
see, lah mangherah estah rrotah

Yes, the hose is broken.

¿La puede arreglar?
lah pweday arreglar

Can you repair it?

4 Useful phrases (3 minutes)

Practise these phrases and then test yourself using the cover flap.

Can you clean the bathroom?	**¿Puede limpiar el cuarto de baño?** _pweday leempyar el kwartoh day banyoh_
Can you repair the boiler?	**¿Puede arreglar la caldera?** _pweday arreglar lah kalderah_
Do you know a good electrician?	**¿Conoce a un buen electricista?** _konothay ah oon bwen ehlektreetheestah_

¿Dónde me pueden arreglar la plancha?
donday may pweden arreglar lah planchah
Where can I get the iron repaired?

5 Put into practice (4 minutes)

Empiezo el trabajo mañana.
empyaythoh el trabahoh manyanah
I start the job tomorrow.

los planos
los planos
plans

Practise these phrases. Cover the text on the right and complete the dialogue in Spanish. Check your answers and repeat if necessary.

Su verja está rota. _soo berhah estah rrotah_ Your gate is broken. Ask: Do you know a good builder?	**¿Conoce a un buen albañil?** _konothay ah oon bwen albanyeel_
Sí, hay uno en el pueblo. _see, ah-ee oonoh en el pwebloh_ Yes, there is one In the village. Ask: Do you have his phone number?	**¿Tiene su número de teléfono?** _tyenay soo noomeroh day telefonoh_

No, va a necesitar una nueva.
noh, bah ah netheseetar oonah nwebah
No, you'll need a new one.

¿Lo puede hacer hoy?
loh pweday ahther oy
Can you do it today?

No, volveré mañana.
noh, bolberay manyanah
No. I'll come back tomorrow.

VENIR
To come

The verb **venir** (*to come*) is one of the most useful verbs. As well as the main verb (see below) it is worth knowing the instruction **¡ven!/¡venga!** (*come here!* informal/formal). Note that *with me* becomes **conmigo** and *with you* **contigo**: **ven conmigo** (*come with me*); **vengo contigo** (*I'm going with you*).

1 Warm up (1 minute)

Say the days of the week in Spanish. (pp.28-9)

How do you say "cleaner"? (pp.110-11)

Say "It's 9.30", "10.45", "12.00". (pp.30-1)

2 Venir: to come (6 minutes)

Say the different forms of the verb aloud, reading from the table. Use the cover flap to test yourself and, when you are confident, practise the sample sentences below.

yo vengo *yoh bengoh*	I come
tú vienes/usted viene *too byenes/oosted byenay*	you come (informal/ formal singular)
él/ella viene *el/eh-yah byenay*	he/she comes
nosotros(-as) venimos *nosotros(-as) beneemos*	we come
vosotros(-as) venís *bosotros(-as) benees*	you come (informal plural)
ustedes vienen *oostedes byenen*	you come (formal plural)
ellos/ellas vienen *eh-yos/eh-yas byenen*	they come

Vengo ahora. *bengoh ah-orah*	I'm coming now.
Venimos todos los martes. *beneemos todos los martes*	We come every Tuesday.
Vienen en tren. *byenen en tren*	They come by train.

Vienen en muchos colores.
beeaynen en moochos kolores
They come in many colours.

Conversational tip To say *I come from England* in Spanish, you have to use the verb *to be*, as in **soy inglés** (*I am from England*). When you use the verb *to come*, as in **Vengo de Londres**, it means you have just arrived from London.

3 Useful phrases (4 minutes)

¿Puede venir el viernes?
pweday beneer el byairnes
Can you come on Friday?

Learn these phrases and then test yourself using the cover flap.

When can I come?	**¿Cuándo puedo venir?** *kwandoh pwedoh beneer*
Does it come in size 44?	**¿Viene en la talla 44?** *byenay en lah tayah kwarentah ee kwatroh*
The cleaner comes every Monday.	**La asistenta viene todos los lunes.** *lah aseestentah byenay todos los loones*
Come with me. (informal/formal)	**Ven conmigo/ Venga conmigo.** *ben konmeegoh/ bengah konmeegoh*

4 Put into practice (4 minutes)

Practise these phrases. Then cover the text on the right and say the anwering part of the dialogue in Spanish. Check your answers and repeat if necessary.

Peluquería Cristina, dígame.
pelookereeah kristeenah, deegamay

Christine's hair salon. Can I help you?

Say: I'd like an appointment.

Quisiera una cita.
keesyairah oonah theetah

¿Cuándo quiere venir?
kwandoh kyairay beneer

When do you want to come?

Say: Today, if possible.

Hoy, si es posible.
oy, see es poseeblay

Sí, claro. ¿A qué hora?
see klaroh, ah kay orah

Yes of course. What time?

Say: At 10.30.

A las diez y media.
ah las dyeth ee medeeah

1 Warm up (1 minute)

What's the Spanish for "big" and "small"? (pp.64-5)

Say "The room is big" and "The bed is small". (pp.64-5)

LA POLICÍA Y EL DELITO
Police and crime

While in Spain, if you are the victim of a crime, you should go to the police station to report it, or in an emergency, you can dial 112. You may have to explain your complaint in Spanish, so some basic vocabulary is useful.

2 Words to remember: crime (4 minutes)

Familiarize yourself with these words.

el robo *el rroboh*	robbery
la denuncia *lah denoontheeah*	police report
el ladrón *el ladron*	thief
la policía *lah poleetheeah*	police
la declaración *lah deklarathyon*	statement
el testigo *el testeegoh*	witness
el abogado *el abogadoh*	lawyer

Necesito un abogado.
netheseetoh oon abogadoh
I need a lawyer.

3 Useful phrases (3 minutes)

Learn these phrases and then test yourself.

Me han robado. *may an rrobadoh*	I've been robbed.
¿Qué han robado? *kay an rrobadoh*	What was stolen?
¿Vió quién lo hizo? *byoh kyain loh eethoh*	Did you see who did it?
¿Cuándo ocurrió? *kwandoh okoorryoh*	When did it happen?

la cámara de fotos
lah kamarah day fotos
camera

la cartera
la karterah
purse

4 Words to remember: appearance (5 minutes)

Learn these words. Remember some adjectives have a feminine form.

man	**el hombre** *el ombray*
woman	**la mujer** *lah moo-hair*
tall	**alto/alta** *altoh/altah*
short	**bajo/baja** *bahoh/bahah*
young	**joven** *hoben*
old	**viejo/vieja** *byayhoh/byayhah*
fat	**gordo/gorda** *gordoh/gordah*
thin	**delgado/delgada** *delgadoh/delgadah*
long/short hair	**el pelo largo/corto** *el peloh largoh/kortoh*
glasses	**las gafas** *las gafas*
beard	**la barba** *la barbah*

Él es bajo y tiene bigote.
el es bahoh ee tyenay beegotay
He is short and has a moustache.

Tiene el pelo negro y corto.
tyenay el peloh negroh ee kortoh
He has short, black hair.

Cultural tip In Spain there is a difference between **la guardia civil** and **la policía**. **La policía** are the local police while **la guardia civil** operates in airports and patrols the national road system. The police uniforms are blue and those of the **guardia civil** are green.

5 Put into practice (2 minutes)

Practise these phrases. Then cover the text on the right and follow the instructions to make your reply in Spanish.

¿Cómo era?   **Bajo y gordo.**
komoh ehrah   *bahoh ee gordoh*

What did he look like?

Say: Short and fat.

¿Y el pelo?   **Largo y con barba.**
ee el peloh   *largoh ee kon barbah*

And his hair?

Say: Long with a beard.

REPASE Y REPITA
Review and repeat

Respuestas
Answers (Cover with flap)

1 To come

❶ **vienen**
byenen

❷ **viene**
byenay

❸ **venimos**
beneemos

❹ **venís**
benees

❺ **vengo**
bengoh

1 To come (3 minutes)

Put the correct form of **venir** (*to come*) in the gaps.

❶ Mis padres _____ a las cuatro.

❷ La asistenta _____ una vez a la semana.

❸ Nosotros _____ todos los martes.

❹ ¿ _____ vosotros con nosotros?

❺ Yo _____ en taxi.

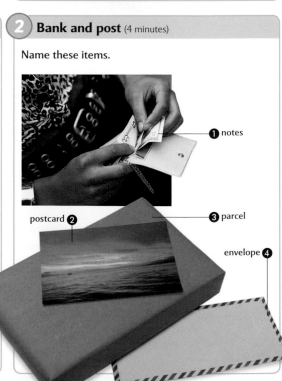

2 Bank and post

❶ **los billetes**
los beeyetes

❷ **la postal**
lah postal

❸ **el paquete**
el paketay

❹ **el sobre**
el sobray

2 Bank and post (4 minutes)

Name these items.

❶ notes

postcard ❷

❸ parcel

envelope ❹

3 Appearance (4 minutes)

What do these descriptions mean?

❶ Es un hombre alto y delgado.
❷ Ella tiene el pelo corto y gafas.
❸ Soy baja y tengo el pelo largo.
❹ Ella es vieja y gorda.
❺ Él tiene los ojos azules y barba.

3 Appearance

❶ He's a tall, thin man.
❷ She has short hair and glasses.
❸ I'm short and I have long hair.
❹ She's old and fat.
❺ He has blue eyes and a beard.

4 The pharmacy (4 minutes)

You are asking a pharmacist for advice. Join in the conversation, replying in Spanish following the English prompts.

Buenos días, ¿qué desea?
❶ I have a cough.

¿Le duele el pecho?
❷ No, but I have a headache.

Tiene estas pastillas.
❸ Do you have that as a syrup?

Sí señor. Aquí tiene.
❹ Thank you. How much is that?

Cuatro euros.
❺ Here you are. Goodbye.

4 The pharmacy

❶ **Tengo tos.**
tengoh tos

❷ **No, pero me duele la cabeza.**
noh, peroh may dwelay lah kabethah

❸ **¿Lo tiene en jarabe?**
loh tyenay en harabay

❹ **Gracias. ¿Cuánto es?**
grathyas. kwantoh es

❺ **Aquí tiene. Adiós.**
ahkee tyenay. addy-os

WEEK 12

EL OCIO
Leisure time

Warm up (1 minute)

What is the Spanish for "museum" and "art gallery"? (pp.48-9)

Say "I don't like the curtains". (pp.100-1)

Ask "Do you want...?" informally. (pp.22-3)

The Spanish pride themselves on their lively nightlife and love for the arts, including theatre and film. It is not unusual for Spaniards to number politics or philosophy among their interests. Be prepared for these topics to be the subject of conversation in social situations.

Words to remember (4 minutes)

Familiarize yourself with these words and test yourself using the cover flap to conceal the Spanish on the left.

el teatro *el te-ahtroh*	theatre
el cine *el theenay*	cinema
la discoteca *lah deeskotekah*	discotheque
el deporte *el deportay*	sport
el turismo *el tooreesmoh*	sightseeing
la política *la poleeteekah*	politics
la música *lah mooseekah*	music
el arte *el artay*	art

Me encanta el baile.
me enkantah el baeelay
I love dancing.

In conversation (4 minutes)

Hola. ¿Quieres jugar al tenis hoy?
o-lah. kyaires hoogar al tenis oy

Hi, do you want to play tennis today?

No, no me gusta el deporte.
noh, noh may goostah el deportay

No, I don't like sport.

Y entonces, ¿qué te gusta?
ee entonthes, kay tay goostah

So then, what do you like?

los video-juegos
los beedayoh-hwegos
video games

la bailadora
lah baeeladorah
dancer

el traje típico
el trahay teepeekoh
traditional costume

4 Useful phrases (4 minutes)

Learn these phrases and then test yourself using the cover flap.

What are your (formal/ informal) interests?	**¿Cuáles son sus/ tus intereses?** *kwales son soos/ toos intereses*
I like the theatre.	**Me gusta el teatro.** *may goostah el te-ahtroh*
I prefer the cinema.	**Yo prefiero el cine.** *yoh prefyairoh el theenay*
I'm interested in art.	**Me interesa el arte.** *may interesah el artay*
That bores me.	**Eso me aburre.** *ehsoh may aboorray*

5 Say it (2 minutes)

I'm interested in music.

I prefer sport.

I don't like video games.

Prefiero el turismo e ir de compras.
prefyairoh el tooreesmoh eh eer day kompras

I prefer sightseeing and shopping.

Eso a mí no me interesa.
ehsoh ah mee noh may interesah

That doesn't interest me.

No pasa nada. Me voy yo sola.
noh pasah nadah. may boy yoh solah

No problem. I'll go on my own.

EL DEPORTE Y LOS PASATIEMPOS
Sport and hobbies

1 Warm up (1 minute)

Ask "Do you (formal) want to play tennis?" (pp.118-19)

Say "I like the theatre" and "I prefer sightseeing". (pp.118-19)

Say "That doesn't interest me". (pp.118-19)

Hacer (*to do* or *to make*) and **jugar** (*to play*) are the verbs used most when talking about sport and pastimes. **Jugar** is followed by **al** when you are talking about playing a sport, as in **juego al baloncesto** (*I play basketball*).

2 Words to remember (5 minutes)

Familiarize yourself with these words and then test yourself.

el fútbol/rugby el <u>foot</u>bol/<u>roog</u>bee	football/rugby
el tenis/baloncesto el <u>ten</u>is/balon<u>thes</u>toh	tennis/basketball
la natación lah natath<u>yon</u>	swimming
la vela lah <u>be</u>lah	sailing
la pesca lah <u>pes</u>kah	fishing
la pintura lah peen<u>too</u>rah	painting
el ciclismo el thee<u>klees</u>moh	cycling
el senderismo el sende<u>rees</u>moh	hiking

el búnker
el bunker
bunker

el jugador de golf
el hugador day golf
golfer

Juego al golf todos los días.
hwegoh al golf todos los deeyas
I play golf every day.

3 Useful phrases (2 minutes)

Learn these phrases and then test yourself.

Juego al fútbol. *hwegoh al <u>foot</u>bol*	I play football.
Juega al tenis. *hwegah al <u>ten</u>is*	He plays tennis.
Ella pinta. *eh-yah <u>peen</u>tah*	She paints.

4 Hacer: to do or to make (4 minutes)

Hacer is a useful verb meaning *to do* or *to make*.
It is commonly used to describe leisure pursuits.
Hace is also used to describe the weather.

I do	**yo hago** *yoh ahgoh*
you do (informal/ formal singular)	**tú haces/usted hace** *too ahthes/oosted ahthay*
he/she does	**él/ella hace** *el/eh-yah ahthay*
we do	**nosotros(-as) hacemos** *nosotros(-as) ahthemos*
you do (informal plural)	**vosotros(-as) hacéis** *bosotros(-as) ahthays*
you do (formal plural)	**ustedes hacen** *oostedes ahthen*
they do	**ellos/ellas hacen** *eh-yos/eh-yas ahthen*
What do you like doing? (informal/formal singular)	**¿Qué te/le gusta hacer?** *kay tay/lay goostah ahthair?*
I go hiking.	**Yo hago senderismo.** *yoh ahgoh sendereesmoh*

Hoy hace bueno.
oy ahthay bwenoh
It's nice (weather) today.

la banderola
lah bandairolah
flag

el campo de golf
el kampoh day golf
golf course

5 Put into practice (3 minutes)

Join in this conversation following the English prompts.

¿Qué te gusta hacer?
kay tay goostah ahthair
What do you like doing?

Say: I like playing tennis.

Me gusta jugar al tenis.
may goostah hoogar al tenis

¿Juegas al fútbol también?
hwegas al footbol tambyen
Do you play football as well?

Say: No, I play rugby.

No, juego al rugby.
noh, hwegoh al roogbee

¿Cuándo juegas?
kwandoh hwegas
When do you play?

Say: I play every week.

Juego todas las semanas.
hwegoh todas las semanas

1 Warm up (1 minute)

Say "my husband" and "my wife". (pp.10-11)

Say the days of the week in Spanish. (pp.28-9)

Say "Sorry, I'm busy". (pp.32-3)

LA VIDA SOCIAL
Socializing

The dinner table is the centre of the Spanish social world. You can expect to do a lot of your socializing around the table, enjoying food and wine. In general it is best to use the more polite **usted** form to talk to older people and **tú** with the younger crowd.

la invitada
lah inbeetadah
guest

2 Useful phrases (3 minutes)

Practise these phrases and then test yourself.

Me gustaría invitarte a cenar. *may goostareeah inbeetartay ah thenar*	I'd like to invite you to dinner.
¿Estás libre el miércoles que viene? *estas leebray el myairkoles kay byenay*	Are you free next Wednesday?
Quizá otro día. *keethah ohtroh deeyah*	Perhaps another day.

Cultural tip When you visit someone's house for the first time, it is usual to bring flowers or wine. If you are invited again, having seen your host's house, you can bring something a little more personal.

3 In conversation (3 minutes)

¿Quieres venir a comer el martes?
kyaires beneer ah komer el martes

Would you like to come to lunch on Tuesday?

Lo siento, estoy ocupada.
loh syaintoh, estoy okoopadah

I'm sorry, I'm busy.

¿Qué tal el jueves?
kay tal el hwebes

What about Thursday?

4 **Words to remember** (3 minutes)

Familiarize yourself with these words and test yourself using the flap.

la anfitriona
lah anfeetryonah
hostess

party	**la fiesta** *lah fyaystah*
dinner party	**la cena** *lah thenah*
invitation	**la invitación** *lah inbeetathyon*
reception	**la recepción** *lah rrethepthyon*
cocktail party	**el coctel** *el koktel*

5 **Put into practice** (5 minutes)

Join this conversation, replying in Spanish.

¿Puede venir a una recepción esta noche?
pweday beneer ah oonah rrethepthyon estah nochay

Can you come to a reception tonight?

Say: Yes, I'd love to.

Sí, encantado/-a.
see, enkan-tadoh/-ah

Empieza a las ocho.
empyaythah ah las ochoh

It starts at eight o'clock.

Ask: What should I wear?

¿Qué me pongo?
kay may pongoh

Gracias por invitarnos.
grathyas por inbeetarnos
Thank you for inviting us.

Encantada.
enkan-tadah

I'd be delighted.

Ven con tu marido.
ben kon too mareedoh

Bring your husband.

Gracias, ¿a qué hora?
grathyas, ah kay orah

Thank you, at what time?

Respuestas
Answers (Cover with flap)

REPASE Y REPITA
Review and repeat

1 Animals

Respuestas
Answers (Cover with flap)

❶ **el pez**
el peth

❷ **el pájaro**
el paharoh

❸ **el conejo**
el konehoh

❹ **el gato**
el gatoh

❺ **el hámster**
el hamster

❻ **el perro**
el perroh

1 Animals (3 minutes)

Name the numbered animals in Spanish.

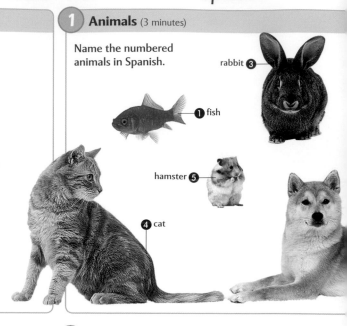

rabbit ❸

❶ fish

hamster ❺

❹ cat

2 I like...

❶ **Me gusta el fútbol.**
may goostah el footbol

❷ **No me gusta el golf.**
noh may goostah el golf

❸ **Me gusta pintar.**
may goostah peentar

❹ **No me gustan las flores.**
noh may goostan las flores

2 I like ... (4 minutes)

Say the following in Spanish:

❶ I like football.
❷ I don't like golf.
❸ I like painting.
❹ I don't like flowers.

2 bird

6 dog

3 Hacer (4 minutes)

Use the correct form of the verb **hacer** (*to do* or *to make*) in these sentences.

❶ Vosotros _____ senderismo.

❷ Ella _____ eso todos los días.

❸ ¿Qué _____ tú?

❹ Hoy no _____ frío.

❺ ¿Qué _____ ellos esta noche?

❻ Yo _____ natación.

3 Hacer

❶ hacéis
ahthays

❷ hace
ahthay

❸ haces
ahthes

❹ hace
ahthay

❺ hacen
ahthen

❻ hago
ahgoh

4 An invitation (4 minutes)

You are invited for dinner. Join in the conversation, replying in Spanish following the English prompts.

¿Quieres venir a comer el viernes?
❶ I'm sorry, I'm busy.

¿Qué tal el sábado?
❷ I'd be delighted.

Ven con los niños.
❸ Thank you. What time?

A las doce y media.
❹ That's good for me.

4 An invitation

❶ Lo siento, estoy ocupado/-a.
loh syentoh, estoy okoopadoh/-ah

❷ Encantado/-a.
enkantadoh/-ah

❸ Gracias. ¿A qué hora?
grathyas. ah kay orah

❹ Me viene bien.
may byenay byen

Reinforce and progress

Regular practice is the key to maintaining and advancing your language skills. In this section you will find a variety of suggestions for reinforcing and extending your knowledge of Spanish. Many involve returning to exercises in the book and using the dictionaries to extend their scope. Go back through the lessons in a different order, mix and match activities to make up your own 15-minute daily programme, or focus on topics that are of particular relevance to your current needs.

1 Warm up (1 minute)

Say "he is" and "they are". (pp.14–15)

Say "he is not" and "they are not". (pp.14–15)

What is Spanish for "the children"? (pp.10–11)

3 I'd like... (3 minutes)

Say "I'd like" the following:

1 black coffee   churros 2   3 sugar

white coffee 4

Keep warmed up
Re-visit the Warm Up boxes to remind yourself of key words and phrases. Make sure you work your way through all of them on a regular basis.

Review and repeat again
Work through a Review and Repeat lesson as a way of reinforcing words and phrases presented in the course. Return to the main lesson for any topic on which you are no longer confident.

3 In conversation: taxi (2 minutes)

Carry on conversing
Re-read the In Conversation panels. Say both parts of the conversation, paying attention to the pronunciation. Where possible, try incorporating new words from the dictionary.

A la Plaza de España, por favor.
ah lah plathah day espanyah, por fabor

Plaza de España, please.

Sí, de acuerdo, señor.
see, day akwairdo, senyor

Yes, certainly, sir.

¿Me puede dejar aquí, por favor?
may pweday dehar ahkee, por fabor

Can you drop me here, please?

3 Useful phrases (5 minutes)

Practise these phrases and then test yourself using the cover flap.

The room is too cold/hot.	**Hace demasiado frío/calor en la habitación.** *ahthay daymasyahdoh freeoh/kalor en lah abeetathyon*
There are no towels.	**No hay toallas.** *noh ah-ee toh-ahyas*
I need some soap.	**Necesito jabón.** *netheseetoh habon*
The shower doesn't work.	**La ducha no funciona.** *lah doochah noh foonthyonah*

Practise phrases
Return to the Useful Phrases and Put into Practice exercises. Test yourself using the cover flap. When you are confident, devise your own versions of the phrases, using new words from the dictionary.

Match, repeat, and extend
Remind yourself of words related to specific topics
by returning to the Match and Repeat and Words
to Remember exercises. Test yourself using the cover
flap. Discover new words in that area by referring
to the dictionary and menu guide.

grapes ④
mushrooms ③
beans ②
① tomatoes
peppers ⑧
⑤ cucumbers
artichokes ⑥
peas ⑦

2 Match and repeat (4 minutes)

Match the numbered items in this scene
with the text in the panel.

① **los tomates**
los to*mates*

② **las judías**
las hoo*dee*as

③ **los champiñones**
los champeen*yo*nes

④ **las uvas**
las *oo*bas

⑤ **los pepinos**
los pe*pee*nos

⑥ **las alcachofas**
las alka*cho*fas

⑦ **los guisantes**
los ghee*san*tes

⑧ **los pimientos**
los peem*yain*tos

5 Say it (2 minutes)

Two kilos of peas, please.
The mushrooms are
too expensive.
How much are
the grapes?

Say it again
The Say It exercises are a useful instant
reminder for each lesson. Practise these,
using your own vocabulary variations from
the dictionary or elsewhere in the lesson.

Using other resources

In addition to working with this
book, try the following language
extension ideas:

Visit a Spanish-speaking country and
try out your new skills with native
speakers. Find out if there is a Spanish
community near you. There may be
shops, cafés, restaurants, and clubs.
Try to visit some of these and use
your Spanish to order food and drink
and strike up conversations. Most
native speakers will be happy to
speak Spanish to you.

Join a language class or club. There
are usually evening and day classes
available at different levels. Or
you could start a club yourself if you
have friends who are also interested
in keeping up their Spanish.

Look at Spanish magazines and
newspapers. The pictures will
help you to understand the text.
Advertisements are also a useful
way of expanding your vocabulary.

Use the Internet, where you can find
all kinds of websites for learning
languages, some of which offer free
online help and activities. You can
also find Spanish websites for
everything from renting a house
to shampooing your pet. You can
even access Spanish radio and TV
stations online. Start by going to
a Spanish search engine, such as
ozu.es, and keying in a hobby or sport
that interests you, or set yourself
a challenge, such as finding a two-
bedroom house for rent in Madrid.

MENU GUIDE

This guide lists the most common terms you may encounter on Spanish menus or when shopping for food. If you can't find an exact phrase, try looking up its component parts.

A

aceitunas *olives*
acelgas *spinach beet*
achicoria *chicory*
aguacate *avocado*
ahumados *smoked*
agua mineral *mineral water*
ajo *garlic*
al ajillo *with garlic*
a la parrilla *grilled*
a la plancha *grilled*
albaricoques *apricots*
albóndigas *meatballs*
alcachofas *artichokes*
alcaparras *capers*
al horno *baked*
allioli *garlic mayonnaise*
almejas *clams*
almejas a la marinera *clams stewed in wine and parsley*
almejas naturales *live clams*
almendras *almonds*
almíbar *syrup*
alubias *beans*
ancas de rana *frogs' legs*
anchoas *anchovies*
anguila *eel*
angulas *baby eels*
arenque *herring*
arroz a la cubana *rice with fried eggs and banana fritters*
arroz a la valenciana *rice with seafood*
arroz con leche *rice pudding*
asados *roast meat*
atún *tuna*
azúcar *sugar*

B

bacalao a la vizcaína *cod served with ham, peppers, and chillies*
bacalao al pil pil *cod served with chillies and garlic*
batido *milk shake*
bebidas *drinks*
berenjenas *aubergine*
besugo al horno *baked sea bream*
bistec de ternera *veal steak*

bonito *fish similar to tuna*
boquerones fritos *fried, fresh anchovies*
brazo gitano *swiss roll*
brocheta de riñones *kidney kebabs*
buñuelos *fried pastries*
butifarra *Catalan sausage*

C

cabrito asado *roast kid*
cacahuetes *peanuts*
cachelada *pork stew with eggs, tomato, and onion*
café *coffee*
café con leche *coffee with steamed milk*
calabacines *courgette*
calabaza *pumpkin*
calamares a la romana *squid rings in batter*
calamares en su tinta *squid cooked in their ink*
caldeirada *fish soup*
caldereta gallega *vegetable stew*
caldo de ... ... *soup*
caldo de gallina *chicken soup*
caldo de pescado *clear fish soup*
caldo gallego *vegetable soup*
caldo guanche *soup of potatoes, tomatoes, onions, and courgettes*
callos a la madrileña *tripe cooked with chillies*
camarones *baby prawns*
canela *cinnamon*
cangrejos *crabs*
caracoles *snails*
caramelos *sweets*
carnes *meats*
castañas *chestnuts*
cebolla *onion*
cebolletas *spring onions*
centollo *spider crab*
cerdo *pork*
cerezas *cherries*
cerveza *beer*
cesta de frutas *selection of fresh fruit*
champiñones *mushrooms*
chanquetes *fish (similar to whitebait)*

chipirones *baby squid*
chipirones en su tinta *squid cooked in their ink*
chocos *cuttlefish*
chorizo *spicy sausage*
chuleta de buey *beef chop*
chuleta de cerdo *pork chop*
chuleta de cerdo empanada *breaded pork chop*
chuleta de cordero *lamb chop*
chuleta de cordero empanada *breaded lamb chop*
chuleta de ternera *veal chop*
chuleta de ternera empanada *breaded veal chop*
chuletas de lomo ahumado *smoked pork chops*
chuletitas de cordero *small lamb chops*
chuletón *large chop*
chuletón de buey *large beef chop*
churros *deep-fried pastry strips*
cigalas *crayfish*
cigalas cocidas *boiled crayfish*
ciruelas *plums*
ciruelas pasas *prunes*
cochinillo asado *roast suckling pig*
cocido *meat, chickpea, and vegetable stew*
cocktail de bogavante *lobster cocktail*
cococha (de merluza) *hake stew*
cóctel de gambas *prawn cocktail*
cóctel de langostinos *jumbo prawn cocktail*
cóctel de mariscos *seafood cocktail*
codornices *quail*
codornices escabechadas *marinated quail*
codornices estofadas *braised quail*
col *cabbage*
coles de Bruselas *Brussels sprouts*
coliflor *cauliflower*
coñac *brandy*
conejo *rabbit*

conejo encebollado rabbit
with onions
congrio conger eel
consomé con yema consommé
with egg yolk
consomé de ave fowl consommé
**contra de ternera con
guisantes** veal stew with peas
contrafilete de ternera
veal fillet
copa glass (of wine)
copa de helado ice cream,
assorted flavours
cordero asado roast lamb
cordero chilindrón lamb
stew with onion, tomato,
peppers, and eggs
costillas de cerdo pork ribs
crema catalana crème brûlée
cremada dessert made with egg,
sugar, and milk
crema de... cream of ... soup
crema de legumbres cream
of vegetable soup
crepe imperiale crêpe suzette
criadillas de tierra truffles
crocante ice cream with
chopped nuts
croquetas croquettes
cuajada curds

D, E

dátiles dates
embutidos sausages
embutidos de la tierra
local sausages
empanada gallega fish pie
empanada santiaguesa fish pie
empanadillas small pies
endivia endive
en escabeche marinated
ensalada salad
ensalada de arenque fish salad
ensalada ilustrada mixed salad
ensalada mixta mixed salad
ensalada simple green salad
ensaladilla rusa Russian salad
(potatoes, carrots, peas, and
other vegetables in mayonnaise)
entrecot a la parrilla
grilled entrecôte
entremeses hors d'oeuvres,
starters
escalope a la milanesa
breaded veal with cheese
escalope a la parrilla
grilled veal
escalope a la plancha
grilled veal
escalope de lomo de cerdo
escalope of pork fillet
escalope de ternera
veal escalope

escalope empanado
breaded escalope
**escalopines al vino de
Marsala** veal escalopes cooked
in Marsala wine
escalopines de ternera
veal escalopes
espadín a la toledana kebab
espaguetis spaghetti
espárragos asparagus
espárragos trigueros wild
green asparagus
espinacas spinach
**espinazo de cerdo con
patatas** stew of pork ribs
with potatoes
estofado braised; stew
estragón tarragon

F

fabada (asturiana) bean stew
with sausage
faisán pheasant
faisán trufado pheasant
with truffles
fiambres cold meats
fideos thin pasta, noodles
filete a la parrilla grilled
beef steak
filete de cerdo pork steak
filete de ternera veal steak
flan crème caramel
frambuesas raspberries
fresas strawberries
fritos fried
fruta fruit

G

gallina en pepitoria chicken
stew with peppers
gambas prawns
gambas cocidas boiled prawns
gambas en gabardina prawns
in batter
gambas rebozadas prawns
in batter
garbanzos chickpeas
garbanzos a la catalana
chickpeas with sausage, boiled
eggs, and pine nuts
gazpacho andaluz cold
tomato soup
gelatina de ... ... jelly
gratén de ... ... au gratin (baked
in a cream and cheese sauce)
granizada crushed ice drink
gratinada/o au gratin
grelo turnip
grillado grilled
guisantes peas
guisantes salteados
sautéed peas

H

habas broad beans
habichuelas white beans
helado ice cream
helado de vainilla vanilla
ice cream
helado de turrón nougat
ice cream
hígado liver
hígado de ternera calves' liver
hígado estofado braised liver
higos con miel y nueces figs
with honey and nuts
higos secos dried figs
horchata (de chufas) cold drink
made from chufa nuts
huevo hilado egg yolk garnish
huevos eggs
huevos a la flamenca fried
eggs with ham, tomato,
and vegetables
huevos cocidos hard-boiled eggs
huevos con patatas fritas
fried eggs and chips
huevos con picadillo eggs with
minced meat
huevos duros hard-boiled eggs
huevos escalfados poached eggs
huevos pasados por agua
soft-boiled eggs
huevos revueltos scrambled
eggs

J

jamón ham
jamón con huevo hilado ham
with egg yolk garnish
jamón serrano cured ham
jarra de vino wine jug
jerez sherry
jeta pigs' cheeks
judías verdes green beans
judías verdes a la española
bean stew
judías verdes al natural plain
green beans
jugo de ... ... juice

L

langosta lobster
langosta a la americana
lobster with brandy and garlic
langosta a la catalana lobster
with mushrooms and ham in
white sauce
langosta fría con mayonesa
cold lobster with mayonnaise
langostinos king prawns
langostinos dos salsas king
prawns cooked in two sauces
laurel bay leaves

leche *milk*

leche frita *pudding made from milk and eggs*

leche merengada *cold milk with meringue*

lechuga *lettuce*

lengua de buey *ox tongue*

lengua de cordero *lambs' tongue*

lenguado a la romana *sole in batter*

lenguado meuniere *sole meunière (floured sole fried in butter)*

lentejas *lentils*

lentejas aliñadas *lentils in vinaigrette dressing*

licores *spirits, liqueurs*

liebre estofada *stewed hare*

lima *lime*

limón *lemon*

lombarda *red cabbage*

lomo curado *pork loin sausage*

lonchas de jamón *sliced, cured ham*

longaniza *cooked Spanish sausage*

lubina *sea bass*

lubina a la marinera *sea bass in a parsley sauce*

M

macedonia de fruta *fruit salad*

mahonesa or mayonesa *mayonnaise*

Málaga *a sweet wine*

mandarinas *tangerines*

manitas de cordero *lamb shank*

manos de cerdo *pigs' feet*

manos de cerdo a la parrilla *grilled pigs' feet*

mantecadas *small sponge cakes*

mantequilla *butter*

manzanas *apples*

mariscada *cold mixed shellfish*

mariscos del día *fresh shellfish*

mariscos del tiempo *seasonal shellfish*

medallones *steaks*

media de agua *half bottle of mineral water*

mejillones *mussels*

mejillones a la marinera *mussels in a wine sauce*

melocotón *peach*

melón *melon*

menestra de legumbres *vegetable stew*

menú de la casa *set menu*

menú del día *set menu*

merluza *hake*

merluza a la cazuela *stewed hake*

merluza al ajo arriero *hake with garlic and chillies*

merluza a la riojana *hake with chillies*

merluza a la romana *hake steaks in batter*

merluza a la vasca *hake in a garlic sauce*

merluza en salsa *hake in sauce*

merluza en salsa verde *hake in a green (parsley and wine) sauce*

merluza fría *cold hake*

merluza frita *fried hake*

mermelada *jam*

mero *grouper (fish)*

mero en salsa verde *grouper in green (garlic and parsley) sauce*

mollejas de ternera fritas *fried sweetbreads*

morcilla *blood sausage*

morcilla de carnero *mutton blood sausage*

morros de cerdo *pigs' cheeks*

morros de vaca *cows' cheeks*

mortadela *salami-type sausage*

morteruelo *kind of pâté*

N, O

nabo *turnip*

naranjas *oranges*

nata *cream*

natillas *cold custard*

níscalos *wild mushrooms*

nueces *walnuts*

orejas de cerdo *pigs' ears*

P

paella *fried rice with seafood and/or meat*

paella castellana *meat paella*

paella valenciana *shellfish, rabbit, and chicken paella*

paleta de cordero lechal *shoulder of lamb*

pan *bread*

panache de verduras *vegetable stew*

panceta *bacon*

parrillada de caza *mixed grilled game*

parrillada de mariscos *mixed grilled shellfish*

pasas *raisins*

pastel de ternera *veal pie*

pasteles *cakes*

patatas a la pescadora *potatoes with fish*

patatas asadas *baked potatoes*

patatas bravas *potatoes in spicy tomato sauce*

patatas fritas *chips*

patitos rellenos *stuffed duckling*

pato a la naranja *duck in orange sauce*

pavo *turkey*

pavo trufado *turkey stuffed with truffles*

pecho de ternera *breast of veal*

pechuga de pollo *breast of chicken*

pepinillos *gherkins*

pepino *cucumber*

peras *pears*

percebes *edible barnacle*

perdices a la campesina *partridges with vegetables*

perdices a la manchega *partridges in red wine, garlic, herbs, and pepper*

perdices escabechadas *marinated partridges*

perejil *parsley*

perritos calientes *hot dogs*

pescaditos fritos *fried fish*

pestiños *sugared pastries flavoured with aniseed*

pez espada *swordfish*

picadillo de ternera *minced veal*

pimienta *black pepper*

pimientos *peppers*

pimientos a la riojana *baked red peppers fried in oil and garlic*

pimientos morrones *a type of bell pepper*

pimientos verdes *green peppers*

piña al gratín *pineapple au gratin*

piña fresca *fresh pineapple*

pinchitos/pinchos *kebabs, snacks served in bars*

pinchos morunos *pork kebabs*

piñones *pine nuts*

pisto *ratatouille*

pisto manchego *vegetable marrow with onion and tomato*

plátanos *bananas*

plátanos flameados *flambéed bananas*

pollo *chicken*

pollo a la riojana *chicken with peppers and chillies*

pollo al ajillo *fried chicken with garlic*

pollo asado *roast chicken*

pollo braseado *braised chicken*

pollo en cacerola *chicken casserole*

pollo en pepitoria *chicken in wine with saffron, garlic, and almonds*

pollos tomateros con zanahorias *young chicken with carrots*

pomelo *grapefruit*

potaje castellano *thick broth*

potaje de ... ... *stew*

puchero canario *casserole of meat, chickpeas, and corn*
pulpitos con cebolla *baby octopus with onions*
pulpo *octopus*
puré de patatas *mashed potatoes, potato purée*
purrusalda *cod with leeks and potatoes*

Q

queso con membrillo *cheese with quince jelly*
queso de bola *Dutch cheese*
queso de Burgos *soft white cheese*
queso del país *local cheese*
queso de oveja *sheep's cheese*
queso gallego *a creamy cheese*
queso manchego *a hard, strong cheese*
quisquillas *shrimps*

R

rábanos *radishes*
ragout de ternera *veal ragoût*
rape a la americana *monkfish with brandy and herbs*
rape a la cazuela *stewed monkfish*
raya *skate*
rebozado *in batter*
redondo al horno *roast fillet of beef*
rellenos *stuffed*
remolacha *beetroot*
repollo *cabbage*
repostería de la casa *cakes baked on the premises*
requesón *cream cheese, cottage cheese*
revuelto de … *scrambled eggs with …*
revuelto de ajos tiernos *scrambled eggs with spring garlic*
revuelto de trigueros *scrambled eggs with asparagus*
revuelto mixto *scrambled eggs with mixed vegetables*
riñones *kidneys*
rodaballo *turbot (fish)*
romero *rosemary*
ron *rum*
roscas *sweet pastries*

S

sal *salt*
salchichas *sausages*
salchichas de Frankfurt *hot dog sausages*

salchichón *sausage similar to salami*
salmón ahumado *smoked salmon*
salmonetes *red mullet*
salmonetes en papillote *red mullet cooked in foil*
salmón frío *cold salmon*
salmorejo *sauce of bread, tomatoes, oil, vinegar, green pepper, and garlic*
salpicón de mariscos *shellfish in vinaigrette*
salsa bechamel *white sauce*
salsa holandesa *hollandaise sauce*
sandía *watermelon*
sardinas a la brasa *barbecued sardines*
seco *dry*
semidulce *medium-sweet*
sesos *brains*
sesos a la romana *fried brains in batter*
sesos rebozados *brains in batter*
setas *mushrooms*
sidra *cider*
sobreasada *sausage with cayenne pepper*
solomillo *fillet steak*
solomillo con patatas *fillet steak with chips*
solomillo de ternera *fillet of veal*
solomillo de vaca *fillet of beef*
solomillo frío *cold roast beef*
sopa *soup*
sopa castellana *vegetable soup*
sopa de almendras *almond soup*
sopa de cola de buey *oxtail soup*
sopa de gallina *chicken soup*
sopa del día *soup of the day*
sopa de legumbres *vegetable soup*
sopa de marisco *fish and shellfish soup*
sopa de rabo de buey *oxtail soup*
sopa mallorquina *soup of tomato, meat, and eggs*
sopa sevillana *fish and mayonnaise soup*
soufflé de fresones *strawberry soufflé*

T

tallarines *noodles*
tallarines a la italiana *tagliatelle*
tarta *cake*
tarta de la casa *cake baked on the premises*

tarta de manzana *apple tart*
tencas *tench*
ternera asada *roast veal*
tocinillos del cielo *a very sweet crème caramel*
tomates *tomatoes*
tomillo *thyme*
torrijas *sweet pastries*
tortilla a la paisana *vegetable omelette*
tortilla a su gusto *omelette made to the customer's wishes*
tortilla de escabeche *fish omelette*
tortilla española *Spanish omelette with potato, onion, and garlic*
tortilla sacromonte *vegetable, brains, and sausage omelette*
tortillas variadas *assorted omelettes*
tournedó *fillet steak*
trucha *trout*
trucha ahumada *smoked trout*
trucha escabechada *marinated trout*
truchas a la marinera *trout in wine sauce*
truchas molinera *trout meunière (floured trout fried in butter)*
trufas *truffles*
turrón *nougat*

U, V

uvas *grapes*
verduras *vegetables*
vieiras *scallops*
vino de mesa/blanco / rosado/tinto *table/ white/rosé/ red wine*

Z

zanahorias a la crema *creamed carrots*
zarzuela de mariscos *seafood stew*
zarzuela de pescados y mariscos *fish and shellfish stew*
zumo de … … *juice*

DICTIONARY
English to Spanish

The gender of a Spanish noun is indicated by the word for *the*: **el** and **la** (masculine and feminine singular) or their plural forms **los** (masculine) and **las** (feminine). Spanish adjectives (adj) vary according to the gender and number of the word they describe, and the masculine form is shown here. In general, adjectives that end in **-o** adopt an **-a** ending in the feminine form, and those that end in **-e** usually stay the same. For the plural form, an **-s** is added.

A

a **un/una**
able: to be able **poder**
about: about sixteen **alrededor de dieciséis**
accelerator **el acelerador**
accident **el accidente**
accommodation **el alojamiento**
accountant **el/la contable**
ache **el dolor**
adaptor **el adaptador**
address **la dirección**
adhesive **el pegamento**
admission charge **el precio de entrada**
after ... **después de ...**
aftershave **el after-shave**
again **otra vez**
against **contra**
agenda **el orden del día**
agency **la agencia**
AIDS **el Sida**
air **el aire**
air conditioning **el aire acondicionado**
aircraft **el avión**
airline **la compañía aérea**
air mail **por avión**
air mattress **la colchoneta**
airport **el aeropuerto**
airport bus **el autobús del aeropuerto**
aisle **el pasillo**
alarm clock **el despertador**
alcohol **el alcohol**
Algeria **Argelia**
all **todo**; *all the streets* **todas las calles**; *that's all* **eso es todo**
allergic **alérgico**
almost **casi**
alone **solo**
already **ya**
always **siempre**
am: I am **soy/estoy**

ambulance **la ambulancia**
America **América**
American **el americano/ la americana**
and **y**; (after 'i' or 'h') **e**
angle-poise lamp **el flexo**
ankle **el tobillo**
another **otro**
answering machine **el contestador automático**
antifreeze **el anticongelante**
antique shop **el anticuario**
antiseptic **el antiséptico**
apartment **el apartamento, el piso**
aperitif **el aperitivo**
appetite **el apetito**
apple **la manzana**
application form **el impreso de solicitud**
appointment (business) **la cita**; (at hairdresser's) **hora**
apricot **el albaricoque**
April **abril**
are: you are (informal singular) **eres/estás**; (formal singular) **es/está**; (informal plural) **sois/ estáis**; (formal plural) **son/están**; *we are* **somos/ estamos**; *they are* **son/están**
arm **el brazo**
arrive **llegar**
art **el arte**
art gallery **la galería de arte**
artichoke **la alcachofa**
artist **el/la artista**
as: as soon as possible **lo antes posible**
ashtray **el cenicero**
asleep: he's asleep **está dormido**
aspirin **la aspirina**
asthmatic **asmático**

at: at the post office **en Correos**; *at night* **por la noche**; *at 3 o'clock* **a las tres**
Atlantic Ocean **el Océano Atlántico**
ATM **el cajero automático**
attic **el ático**
attractive (person) **guapo**; (object) **bonito**; (offer) **atractivo**
aubergines **las berenjenas**
August **agosto**
aunt **la tía**
Australia **Australia**
Australian **el australiano/ la australiana**; (adj) **australiano**
automatic **automático**
available **disponible**
away: is it far away? **¿está lejos?**; *go away!* **¡váyase!**
awful **horrible**
axe **el hacha**
axle **el eje**

B

baby **el niño pequeño, el bebé**
baby wipes **las toallitas para bebé**
back (not front) **la parte de atrás**; (body) **la espalda**
backpack **la mochila**
bacon **el bacon**; *bacon and eggs* **los huevos fritos con bacon**
bad **malo**
bag **la bolsa**
bait **el cebo**
bake **cocer al horno**
bakery **la panadería**
balcony **el balcón**
Balearic Islands **las (Islas) Baleares**
ball (football) **el balon**; (tennis etc) **la pelota**

ballpoint pen **el bolígrafo**
banana **el plátano**
band (musicians) **la banda**
bandage **la venda**
bank **el banco**
bank card **la tarjeta de banco**
banknote **el billete de banco**
bar (drinks) **el bar**
barbecue **la barbacoa**
barber **la peluquería de caballeros**
bargain **la ganga**
basement **el sótano**
basin (sink) **el lavabo**
basket **el cesto**
basketball **el baloncesto**
bath **el baño;** *to have a bath* **darse un baño**
bathing suit **el bañador, el traje de baño**
bathroom **el cuarto de baño**
battery (car) **la batería;** (torch etc) **la pila**
Bay of Biscay **el Golfo de Vizcaya**
be **ser/estar**
beach **la playa**
beach ball **el balón de playa**
beans **las judías**
beard **la barba**
beautiful (object) **precioso;** (person) **guapo**
beauty products **los productos de belleza**
because **porque**
bed **la cama**
bed linen **la ropa de cama**
bedroom **el dormitorio**
bedside lamp **la lamparilla de noche**
bedside table **la mesilla de noche**
bedspread **la colcha**
beef **la carne de vaca**
beer **la cerveza**
before **... antes de ...**
beginner **el/la principiante**
behind **... detrás de ...**
beige **beige**
bell (church) **la campana;** (door) **el timbre**
below **debajo de**
belt **el cinturón**
beside **al lado de**
best **(el) mejor**
better **mejor**
between **entre**
bicycle **la bicicleta**
big **grande**
bill **la cuenta**
bin **el contenedor de basura**

bin liner **la bolsa de basura**
bird **el pájaro**
birthday **el cumpleaños;** *happy birthday!* **¡felicidades!**
birthday present **el regalo de cumpleaños**
biscuit **la galleta**
bite (by dog) **la mordedura;** (by insect) **la picadura;** (verb: by dog) **morder;** (by insect) **picar**
black **negro**
blackberries **las moras**
blackcurrants **las grosellas negras**
blanket **la manta**
bleach **la lejía;** (verb: hair) **teñir**
blind (cannot see) **ciego**
blinds **las persianas**
blister **la ampolla**
blizzard **la ventisca**
blond(e) (adj) **rubio**
blood **la sangre**
blood test **el análisis de sangre**
blouse **la blusa**
blue **azul**
boarding pass **la tarjeta de embarque**
boat **el barco;** (small) **la barca**
body **el cuerpo**
boil (verb: water) **hervir;** (egg etc) **cocer**
boiled **hervido**
bolt (on door) **el cerrojo;** (verb) **echar el cerrojo**
bone **el hueso**
bonnet (car) **el capó**
book **el libro;** (verb) **reservar**
bookshop **la librería**
boot (footwear) **la bota;** (car) **el maletero**
border **el borde;** (between countries) **la frontera**
boring **aburrido**
born: I was born in ... **nací en ...**
both: both of them **los dos;** *both of us* **los dos;** *both ... and ...* **tanto ... como ...**
bottle **la botella**
bottle opener **el abrebotellas**
bottom **el fondo;** (part of body) **el trasero**
bowl **el cuenco**
box **la caja**
box office **la taquilla**
boy **el chico**
boyfriend **el novio**

bra **el sostén**
bracelet **la pulsera**
braces (clothing) **los tirantes**
brake **el freno;** (verb) **frenar**
branch (of company) **la oficina**
brandy **el coñac**
bread **el pan**
breakdown (car) **la avería;** (nervous) **la crisis nerviosa;** *I've had a breakdown* (car) **he tenido una avería**
breakfast **el desayuno**
breathe **respirar**
bridge **el puente;** (game) **el bridge**
briefcase **la cartera**
British **británico**
brochure **el folleto**
broken **roto**
brooch **el broche**
brother **el hermano**
brown **marrón;** (hair) **castaño;** (skin) **moreno**
bruise **el cardenal**
brush (paint) **la brocha;** (cleaning) **el cepillo;** (hair) **el cepillo del pelo;** (verb: hair) **cepillar el pelo**
budget **el presupuesto**
bucket **el cubo**
builder **el albañil**
building **el edificio**
bull **el toro**
bullfight **la corrida de toros**
bullfighter **el torero**
bullring **la plaza de toros**
bumper **el parachoques**
burglar **el ladrón**
burn **la quemadura;** (verb) **quemar**
bus **el autobús**
business **el negocio;** *it's none of your business* **no es asunto suyo**
business card **la tarjeta de vista**
bus station **la estación de autobuses**
busy (bar) **concurrido;** (engaged) **ocupado**
but **pero**
butcher's **la carnicería**
butter **la mantequilla**
button **el botón**
buy **comprar**
by: by the window **junto a la ventana;** *by Friday* **para el viernes;** *by myself* **yo solo;** *written by* **escrito por**

C

cabbage la col
cable car el teleférico
cable TV la television
  por cable
café el café
cage la jaula
cake (small) el pastel;
  (large) la tarta;
  sponge cake el bizcocho
cake shop la pastelería
calculator la calculadora
call: what's it called?
  ¿cómo se llama?
camcorder la videocámara
camera la máquina de
  fotos, la cámara de fotos
camper van la autocaravana
campfire la hoguera
camping gas el camping-gas
campsite el camping
camshaft el árbol de levas
can (tin) la lata; (verb: to be
  able) poder; can you ...?
  ¿puede ...?; I can't ...
  no puedo ...
Canada Canadá
Canadian canadiense
canal el canal
Canaries las (Islas) Canarias
candle la vela
can opener el abrelatas
cap (bottle) el tapón; (hat)
  la gorra
car el coche
caravan la roulotte
carburetor el carburador
card la tarjeta
cardigan la rebeca
careful prudente;
  be careful! ¡cuidado!
caretaker el portero,
  el encargado
car park el aparcamiento
carpenter el carpintero
carpet la alfombra
carriage (train) el vagón
carrot la zanahoria
car seat (for baby/child)
  el asiento infantil
case (suitcase) la maleta
cash el dinero; cobrar
  (verb); to pay cash pagar
  al contado
cashier el cajero
cashpoint el cajero
  automático
cassette la cassette, la cinta
cassette player el cassette

castanets las castañuelas
Castile Castilla
Castilian castellano
castle el castillo
cat el gato
Catalonia Cataluña
catch (bus etc) coger
cathedral la catedral
Catholic (adj) católico
cauliflower la coliflor
cave la cueva
ceiling el techo
cellar la bodega
cemetery el cementerio
central heating
  la calefacción central
centre el centro
certificate el certificado
chair la silla
change (money) el cambio;
  (verb: money) cambiar;
  (clothes) cambiarse;
  (trains etc) hacer
  transbordo
charger el cargador
check-in (desk)
  la (el mostrador de)
  facturación
check in (verb) facturar
check-out (supermarket)
  la caja
cheers! (toast) ¡salud!
cheese el queso
chemist la farmacia
cheque el cheque
chequebook el talonario
  de cheques
cherry la cereza
chess el ajedrez
chest (part of body) el pecho;
  (furniture) el arcón
chest of drawers la cómoda
chewing gum el chicle
chicken el pollo
child el niño/la niña
children los niños
children's ward
  la sala de pediatría
chimney la chimenea
china la porcelana
chips las patatas fritas
chocolate el chocolate;
  box of chocolates la caja de
  bombones; chocolate bar
  la tableta de chocolate
chop la chuleta;
  (verb: cut) cortar
Christmas la navidad
church la iglesia
cigar el puro
cigarette el cigarrillo

cinema el cine
city la ciudad
city centre el centro
class la clase
classical music
  la música clásica
clean (adj) limpio
cleaner la asistenta
clear (obvious) evidente;
  (water) claro
clever listo
client el cliente
clock el reloj
close (near) cerca; (stuffy)
  sofocante; (verb) cerrar
closed cerrado
clothes la ropa
clubs (cards) tréboles
coat el abrigo
coat hanger la percha
cockroach la cucaracha
cocktail party el coctel
coffee el café
coin la moneda
cold (illness) el resfriado;
  (adj) frío; I have a cold
  tengo un resfriado;
  I'm cold tengo frío
collar el cuello; (of animal)
  el collar
collection (stamps etc)
  la colección; (postal)
  la recogida
colour el color
colour film la película en color
comb el peine; (verb) peinar
come venir; I come from ...
  soy de ...; we came
  last week llegamos
  la semana pasada;
  come here! ¡venga aquí!
come back volver
compact disc
  el disco compacto
compartment
  el compartimento
complicated complicado
computer el ordenador
computer games
  los vídeo-juegos
concert el concierto
conditioner (hair)
  el acondicionador
condom el condón
conductor (bus) el cobrador;
  (orchestra) el director
conference la conferencia
conference room la sala de
  conferencias
congratulations!
  ¡enhorabuena!

consulate el consulado
contact lenses
　las lentes de contacto
contraceptive el anticonceptivo
contract el contrato
cook el cocinero/la
　cocinera; (verb) guisar
cooker la cocina
cooking utensils los utensilios
　de cocina
cool fresco
cork el corcho
corkscrew el sacacorchos
corner (of street) la esquina;
　(of room) el rincón
corridor el pasillo
cosmetics los cosméticos
cost (verb) costar; what does
　it cost? ¿cuánto cuesta?
cot la cuna
cotton el algodón
cotton wool el algodón
cough la tos; (verb) toser
cough drops las pastillas
　para la garganta
country (state) el país
countryside el campo
cousin el primo/la prima
crab el cangrejo
cramp el calambre
crayfish las cigalas
cream (dairy) la nata;
　(lotion) la crema
credit card la tarjeta
　de crédito
crib el capazo
crisps las patatas fritas
crowded lleno
cruise el crucero
crutches las muletas
cry (weep) llorar;
　(shout) gritar
cucumber el pepino
cuff links los gemelos
cup la taza
cupboard el armario
curlers los rulos
curls los rizos
curry el curry
curtain la cortina
cushion el cojín
customs la aduana
cut la cortadura; (verb) cortar
cycling el ciclismo

D

dad papá
dairy products
　los productos lácteos
damp húmedo

dance el baile; (verb) bailar
dangerous peligroso
dark oscuro; dark blue
　azul oscuro
daughter la hija
day el día
dead muerto
deaf sordo
dear (person) querido
December diciembre
deck of cards la baraja
decorator el pintor
deep profundo
delayed retrasado
deliberately a propósito
delicatessen la charcutería
delivery la entrega
dentist el/la dentista
dentures la dentadura postiza
deny negar
deodorant el desodorante
department el departamento
department store
　los grandes almacenes
departure la salida
departures las salidas
deposit la señal
designer el diseñador/
　la diseñadora
desk la mesa de escritorio
dessert el postre
develop (film) revelar
diabetic diabético
diamonds (jewels) los
　diamantes; (cards)
　los diamantes
diarrhoea la diarrea
diary la agenda
dictionary el
　diccionario
die morir
diesel (oil) fuel-oil;
　(adj: engine) diesel
different diferente; that's
　different! ¡eso es distinto!;
　I'd like a different one
　quisiera otro distinto
difficult difícil
dining room el comedor
dinner la cena
dinner party la cena
dirty sucio
disabled minusválido
discount el descuento
dish cloth el paño de cocina
dishwasher el lavavajillas
disposable nappies
　pañales desechables
divorced divorciado
do hacer
dock el muelle

doctor el médico/la médica
document el documento
dog el perro
doll la muñeca
dollar el dólar
door la puerta
double room
　la habitación doble
doughnut el dónut
down hacia abajo
drawing pin la chincheta
dress el vestido
drink la bebida; (verb)
　beber; would you like
　something to drink?
　¿quiere beber algo?
drinking water agua potable
drive (verb) conducir
driver el conductor
driving licence el carnet
　de conducir
drops las gotas
drunk borracho
dry seco; (sherry) fino
dry cleaner la tintorería
during durante
dustbin el cubo de la basura
duster el trapo del polvo
duty-free libre de Impuestos;
　duty-free shop el duty-free
duvet el edredón

E

each (every) cada;
　20 euros each
　veinte euros cada uno
ear (inner) el oído; (outer)
　la oreja; ears las orejas
early temprano
earrings los pendientes
east este; the East el Este
easy fácil
eat comer
egg el huevo
eight ocho
eighteen dieciocho
eighty ochenta
either: either of them
　cualquiera de ellos; either
　... or ... o bien ... o ...
elastic elástico
elbow el codo
electric eléctrico
electrician el/la electricista
electricity la electricidad
eleven once
else: something else algo más;
　someone else alguien más;
　somewhere else en otro sitio
email el email, el correo

electrónico
email address **la dirección de email**
embarrassing **embarazoso**
embassy **la embajada**
embroidery **el bordado**
emergency **la emergencia**
emergency brake (train) el **freno de emergencia**
emergency department el **servicio de urgencias**
emergency exit **la salida de emergencia**
employee **el empleado**
empty **vacío**
end **el final**
engaged (marriage) **prometido/prometida**; (telephone) **ocupado**
engine (motor) **el motor**
engineering **la ingeniería**
England **Inglaterra**
English **inglés**
Englishman **el inglés**
Englishwoman **la inglesa**
enlargement **la ampliación**
enough **bastante**
entertainment **las diversiones**
entrance **la entrada**
envelope **el sobre**
epileptic **epiléptico**
eraser **la goma de borrar**
escalator **la escalera mecánica**
especially **sobre todo**
espresso **el café solo**
estimate **el presupuesto**
evening **la tarde**
every **cada**; every day **todos los días**
everyone **todos**
everything **todo**
everywhere **por todas partes**
example **el ejemplo**; for example **por ejemplo**
excellent **excelente**
excess baggage **exceso de equipaje**
exchange (verb) **cambiar**
exchange rate **el cambio**
excursion **la excursión**
excuse me! (to get attention) **¡oiga, por favor!**; (when sneezing etc) **¡perdón!**; excuse me, please (to get past) **¿me hace el favor?**
executive **el ejecutivo**
exhaust **el tubo de escape**
exhibition **la exposición**
exit **la salida**

expensive **caro**
extension cord **el cable alargador**
eye **el ojo**
eyebrow **la ceja**

F

face **la cara**
faint (unclear) **tenue**; (verb) **desmayarse**; I feel faint **estoy mareado**
fair **la feria**; it's not fair **no hay derecho**
false teeth **la dentadura postiza**
family **la familia**
fan (enthusiast) **el fan**; (football) **el hincha**; (ventilator) **el ventilador**; (handheld) **el abanico**
fantastic **fantástico**
far **lejos**; how far is it to ...? **¿qué distancia hay a ...?**
fare **el billete, la tarifa**
farm **la granja**
farmer **el granjero**
fashion **la moda**
fast **rápido**
fat (adj) **gordo**; (on meat) **la grasa**
father **el padre**
February **febrero**
feel (touch) **tocar**; I feel hot **tengo calor**; I feel like ... **me apetece ...**; I don't feel well **no me encuentro bien**
felt-tip pen **el rotulador**
fence **la cerca**
ferry **el ferry**
fiancé **el prometido**
fiancée **la prometida**
field (of grass etc) **el campo**; (of study) **la especialidad**
fifteen **quinze**
fifty **cincuenta**
fig **el higo**
figures **los números**
filling (in tooth) **el empaste**; (in sandwich, cake) **el relleno**
film **la película**
filter **el filtro**
filter papers **los papeles de filtro**
finger **el dedo**
fire **el fuego**; (blaze) **el incendio**

fire extinguisher **el extintor**
fireplace **la chimenea**
fireworks **los fuegos artificiales**
first **primero**; first aid **primeros auxilios**
first class **de primera**
first floor **el primer piso**
first name **el nombre de pila**
fish **el pez**; (food) **el pescado**
fishing **la pesca**; to go fishing **ir a pescar**
fishmonger's **la pescadería**
five **cinco**
fizzy water **el agua con gas**
flag **la bandera**
flash (camera) **el flash**
flat (level) **plano**
flat tyre **la rueda pinchada**
flavour **el sabor**
flea **la pulga**
flea spray **el spray antipulgas**
flight **el vuelo**
floor **el suelo**; (storey) **el piso**
flour **la harina**
flower **la flor**
flowerbed **el parterre**
flute **la flauta**
fly (insect) **la mosca**; (verb: of plane, insect) **volar**; (of person) **viajar en avión**
flyover **el paso elevado**
fog **la niebla**
folk music **la música folklórica**
food **la comida**
food poisoning **la intoxicación alimenticia**
foot **el pie**
football **el fútbol**; (ball) **el balón**
for: for me **para mí**; what for? **¿para qué?**; for a week **(para) una semana**
foreigner **el extranjero/la extranjera**
forest **el bosque**; (tropical) **la selva**
forget **olvidar**
fork **el tenedor**; (garden) **la horca**
forty **cuarenta**
fountain **la fuente**
fountain pen **la (pluma) estilográfica**
four **cuatro**
fourteen **catorce**
fourth **cuarto**
France **Francia**
free (not engaged) **libre**; (no charge) **gratis**

freezer el congelador
French francés
Friday viernes
fridge el frigorífico
fried frito
friend el amigo/la amiga
friendly simpático
fringe (hair) el flequillo
front: in front of ...
delante de ...
frost la escarcha
frozen foods los congelados
fruit la fruta
fruit juice el zumo de frutas
fry freír
frying pan la sartén
full lleno; I'm full
(up) estoy lleno
full board pensión completa
funny divertido; (odd) raro
furniture los muebles

G

garage (for parking) el garage;
(for repairs) el taller
garden el jardín
garden centre el vivero
garlic el ajo
gas-permeable lenses
las lentes de contacto
semi-rígidas
gate la puerta, la verja;
(at airport) la puerta
de embarque
gay (homosexual) gay
gearbox la caja de cambios
gear stick la palanca
de velocidades
gel (hair) el gel
German alemán
Germany Alemania
get (fetch) traer; have you
got ...? ¿tiene ...?; to get
the train coger el tren
get back: we get back tomorrow
nos volvemos mañana;
to get something back
recobrar algo
get in (of train etc) subirse;
(of person) llegar
get off (bus etc) bajarse
get on (bus etc) subirse
get out bajarse;
(bring out) sacar
get up (rise) levantarse
Gibraltar Gibraltar
gift el regalo
gin la ginebra
ginger (spice) el jengibre
girl la chica

girlfriend la novia
give dar
glad alegre
glass (material) el cristal;
(for drinking) el vaso,
la copa
glasses las gafas
gloss prints las copias
con brillo
gloves los guantes
glue el pegamento
go ir
gold el oro
good bueno; good! ¡bien!
good afternoon buenas tardes
goodbye adiós
good evening buenas noches
good morning buenos días
government el gobierno
granddaughter la nieta
grandfather el abuelo
grandmother la abuela
grandparents los abuelos
grandson el nieto
grapes las uvas
grass la hierba
Great Britain Gran Bretaña
green verde
greengrocer's la verdulería
grey gris
grill la parrilla
grilled a la plancha
grocer's el ultramarinos,
la tienda de comestibles
ground floor la planta baja
groundsheet la lona
impermeable,
el suelo aislante
guarantee la garantía;
(verb) garantizar
guest la invitada
guide el/la guía
guide book la guía turística
guided tour la visita con guía
guitar la guitarra
gun (rifle) la escopeta;
(pistol) la pistola

H

hair el pelo
haircut el corte de pelo
hairdresser's la peluquería
hairdryer el secador (de pelo)
hairspray la laca
half medio;
half an hour media hora
half board media pensión
ham el jamón
hamburger la hamburguesa
hammer el martillo

hamster el hámster
hand la mano
handbag el bolso
handbrake el freno de mano
handle (door) el picaporte
hand luggage
el equipaje de mano
handshake
el apretón de manos
handsome guapo
hangover la resaca
happy contento, feliz
harbour el puerto
hard duro; (difficult) difícil
hardware store la ferretería
hat el sombrero;
(woollen) el gorro
have tener; I don't have ... no
tengo ...; do you have ...?
¿tiene ...?; I have to go
tengo que irme ; can I
have ...? ¿me pone ...?
hay fever la fiebre del heno
he él
head la cabeza
headache el dolor de cabeza
headlights los faros
headphones los auriculares
hear oír
hearing aid el audífono
heart el corazón
hearts (cards) los corazones
heater la estufa
heating la calefacción
heavy pesado
hedge el seto
heel el talón; (shoe) el tacón
hello hola; (on phone) dígame
help la ayuda; (verb) ayudar
hepatitis la hepatitis
her: it's for her es para ella;
her book su libro; her shoes
sus zapatos; it's hers es
suyo; give it to her déselo
high alto
highway code el código
de la circulación
hiking el senderismo
hill el monte
him: it's for him es para él;
give it to him déselo
hire (verb) alquilar
his: his book su libro; his shoes
sus zapatos; it's his es suyo
history la historia
hitchhike hacer auto-stop
HIV positive seropositivo
hobby el hobby
holiday las vacaciones
home la casa;
at home en casa

homeopathy la homeopatía
honest honrado;
  (sincere) sincero
honey la miel
honeymoon el viaje de novios
horn (car) el claxon; (animal)
  el cuerno
horrible horrible
hospital el hospital
hostess la anfitriona
hour la hora
house la casa
household products los
  productos del hogar
hovercraft el aerodeslizador
how? ¿cómo?
how are you? ¿qué tal?
hundred cien
hungry: I'm hungry
  tengo hambre
hurry: I'm in a hurry
  tengo prisa
husband el marido
hydrofoil la hidroaleta

I

I yo
ice el hielo
ice cream el helado
ice skates
  los patines para hielo
if si
ignition el encendido
immediately inmediatamente
impossible imposible
in en; *in English* en inglés; *in
  the hotel* en el hotel; *in
  Barcelona* en Barcelona;
  he's not in no está
included incluido
indicator el intermitente
indigestion indigestión
inexpensive barato
infection la infección
information la
  información
inhaler (for asthma etc)
  el spray, el inhalador
injection la inyección
injury la herida
ink la tinta
inn la fonda
inner tube
  la cámara (neumática)
insect el insecto
insect repellent
  la loción anti-mosquitos
insomnia el insomnio
instant coffee
  el café instantáneo

insurance el seguro
interesting interesante
internet el internet
interpret interpretar
interpreter el/la
  intérprete
invitation la invitación
invoice la factura
Ireland Irlanda
Irish irlandés/ irlandesa
iron (metal) el hierro;
  (for clothes) la plancha;
  (verb) planchar
is es/está
island la isla
it lo/la
Italian (adj) italiano/
  italiana (m/f)
Italy Italia
its su

J

jacket la chaqueta
jam la mermelada
January enero
jazz el jazz
jeans los tejanos,
  los vaqueros
jellyfish la medusa
jeweller's la joyería
job el trabajo
jog (verb) hacer
  footing
joke la broma;
  (funny story) el chiste
journey el viaje
juice el zumo
July julio
June junio
just (only) sólo; *it's just arrived*
  acaba de llegar

K

kettle el hervidor
  de agua
key la llave
keyboard el teclado
kidney el riñón
kilo el kilo
kilometre el kilómetro
kitchen la cocina
knee la rodilla
knife el cuchillo
knit hacer punto
knitwear los artículos
  de punto
know saber; (person,
  place) conocer;
  I don't know no sé

L

label la etiqueta
lace el encaje
laces (shoe) los cordones
  (de los zapatos)
lady la señora
lake el lago
lamb el cordero
lamp la lámpara, el flexo
lampshade la pantalla
land la tierra;
  (verb) aterrizar
language el idioma
large grande
last (final) último;
  at last! ¡por fin! ; *last week*
  la semana pasada
late: it's getting late se está
  haciendo tarde; *the bus is
  late* el autobús se
  ha retrasado
later más tarde
laugh reír
laundrette la lavandería
  automática
laundry (dirty) la ropa sucia;
  (washed) la colada
law el derecho
lawn el césped
lawn mower la maquina
  cortacésped
lawyer el abogado/
  la abogada
laxative el laxante
lazy perezoso
lead la correa
leaf la hoja
leaflet el folleto
learn aprender
leather el cuero
lecture theatre el anfiteatro
lecturer (university)
  el profesor/la profesora
  de universidad
left (not right) izquierdo;
  there's nothing left
  no queda nada
leg la pierna
lemon el limón
lemonade la limonada
length la longitud
lens la lente
less menos
lesson la clase
letter (mail) la carta;
  (of alphabet) la letra
lettuce la lechuga
library la biblioteca
licence el permiso
life la vida

lift el ascensor
light la luz; (weight) ligero; (not dark) claro
light bulb la bombilla
lighter el encendedor
lighter fuel el gas para el encendedor
light meter el fotómetro
like: I like ... me gusta ...; *I like swimming* me gusta nadar; *it's like ...* es como ...; *like this one* como éste
lime (fruit) la lima
line la cola; (phone etc) línea; (verb) hacer cola
lipstick la barra de labios
liqueur el licor
list la lista
literature la literatura
litre el litro
litter la basura
little (small) pequeño; *it's a little big* es un poco grande; *just a little* sólo un poquito
liver el hígado
living room el cuarto de estar
lobster la langosta
lollipop el chupa-chups
long largo
lost property office la oficina de objetos perdidos
lot: a lot mucho
loud alto
lounge (in house) el cuarto de estar; (in hotel etc) el salón
love el amor; (verb) querer; *I love Spain* me encanta España
lover el/la amante
low bajo
luck: good luck! ¡suerte!
luggage el equipaje
luggage rack la rejilla de equipajes
lunch la comida

M

mad loco
madam señora
magazine la revista
mail el correo
main course el plato principal
main road la calle principal
Majorca Mallorca
make hacer
make-up el maquillaje
man el hombre

manager el/la gerente, el jefe; (hotel) el director/la directora
many muchos/muchas; *many thanks* muchas gracias; *many people* mucha gente; *how many* ¿cuántos?; *too many* demasiados; *not many* no muchos
map el mapa; *town map/plan* el plano
marble el mármol
March marzo
margarine la margarina
market el mercado
marmalade la mermelada de naranja
married casado
mascara el rímel
mass (church) la misa
match (light) la cerilla; (sport) el partido
material (cloth) la tela
matter: it doesn't matter no importa
mattress el colchón
May mayo
maybe quizás
me: it's for me es para mí; *give it to me* démelo
meal la comida
mean: what does this mean? ¿qué significa esto?
meat la carne
mechanic el mecánico
medicine la medicina
Mediterranean el Mediterráneo
medium (sherry) amontillado
medium-dry (wine) semi-seco
meeting la reunión
melon el melón
menu la carta; *set menu* el menú (del día)
message el recado, el mensaje
metro station le estación de metro
microwave el microondas
midday el mediodía
middle: in the middle en el centro
midnight medianoche
milk la leche
mine: it's mine es mío
mineral water el agua mineral
minute el minuto
mirror el espejo
Miss Señorita

mistake la equivocación
mobile phone el teléfono móvil, el teléfono celular
modem el modem
Monday lunes
money el dinero
monitor el monitor
month el mes
monument el monumento
moon la luna
moped el ciclomotor
more más
morning la mañana; *in the morning* por la mañana
Morocco Marruecos
mosaic el mosaico
mosquito el mosquito
mother la madre
motorboat la motora
motorcycle la motocicleta
motorway la autopista
mountain la montaña
mountain bike la bicicleta de montaña
mouse el ratón
mousse (for hair) la espuma moldeadora
moustache el bigote
mouth la boca
move (verb: something) mover; (oneself) moverse; (house) mudarse de casa; *don't move!* ¡no se mueva!
movie la película
Mr Señor
Mrs Señora
much: much better mucho mejor; *much slower* mucho más despacio
mug la jarrita
Mum mama
museum el museo
mushrooms los champiñones, las setas
music la música
musical instrument el instrumento musical
musician el músico
music system el equipo de música
mussels los mejillones
must (to have to) tener que *I must ...* tengo que ...
mustard la mostaza
my: my book mi libro; *my keys* mis llaves

N

nail (metal) **el clavo**; (finger) **la uña**
nail clippers **el cortauñas**
nailfile **la lima de uñas**
nail polish **el esmalte de uñas**
name **el nombre**; what's your name? **¿cómo se llama usted?**; my name is... **me llamo...**
napkin **la servilleta**
nappy **el pañal**
narrow **estrecho**
near: near the door **junto a la puerta**; near New York **cerca de New York**
necessary **necesario**
neck **el cuello**
necklace **el collar**
need (verb) **necesitar**; I need ... **necesito ...**; there's no need **no hace falta**
needle **la aguja**
negative (photo) **el negativo**
neither: neither of them **ninguno de ellos**; neither ... nor ... **ni ... ni ...**
nephew **el sobrino**
never **nunca**
new **nuevo**
news **las noticias**
newsagent's **el kiosko de periódicos**
newspaper **el periódico**
New Zealand **Nueva Zelanda**
New Zealander **el neozelandés/ la neozelandesa**
next **próximo, siguiente**; next week **la semana que viene**; what next? **¿y ahora qué?**
nice **bonito**; (pleasant) **agradable**; (to eat) **bueno**
niece **la sobrina**
night **la noche**
nightclub **la discoteca**
nightgown **el camisón**
night porter **el vigilante nocturno**
nine **nueve**
nineteen **diecinueve**
ninety **noventa**
no (response) **no**; I have no money **no tengo dinero**
nobody **nadie**
noisy **ruidoso**
noon **mediodía**
north **el norte**
Northern Ireland **Irlanda del Norte**
nose **la nariz**
not **no**; he's not ... **no es/está ...**
notebook **el cuaderno**
notepad **el bloc**
nothing **nada**
novel **la novela**
November **noviembre**
now **ahora**
nowhere **en ninguna parte**
nudist **el/la nudista**
number **el número**
number plate **la matrícula**
nurse **el enfermo/la enferma**
nut (fruit) **la nuez**; (for bolt) **la tuerca**

O

oars **los remos**
occasionally **de vez en cuando**
occupied **ocupado**
October **octubre**
octopus **el pulpo**
of **de**
office (place) **la oficina**; (room) **el despacho**
office block **el bloque de oficinas**
often **a menudo**
oil **el aceite**
ointment **la pomada**
OK **vale**
old **viejo**; how old are you? **¿cuántos años tiene?**
olive **la aceituna**
olive oil **el aceite de oliva**
olive tree **el olivo**
omelette **la tortilla**
on ... **en ...**
one **uno**
onion **la cebolla**
only **sólo**
open (adj) **abierto**; (verb) **abrir**
opening times **el horario de apertura**
operating theatre **el quirófano**
operation **la operación**
operator **la operadora**
opposite: opposite the hotel **enfrente del hotel**
optician **el/la oculista**
or **o**
orange (fruit) **la naranja**; (colour) **naranja**
orchestra **la orquesta**
order **el pedido**
organ (music) **el órgano**

other: the other (one) **el otro**
our **nuestro**; it's ours **es nuestro**
out: he's out **no está**
outside **fuera**; external **externa**
oven **el horno**
over ... **encima de ...**; (more than) **más de ...**; it's over the road **está al otro lado de la calle**; when the party is over **cuando termine la fiesta**; over there **allí**
overtake (in car) **adelantar**
oyster **la ostra**

P

package **el paquete**
packet **el paquete**; (cigarettes) **la cajetilla**; (sweets, crisps) **la bolsa**
padlock **el candado**
page **la página**
pain **el dolor**
paint **la pintura**
pair **el par**
palace **el palacio**
pale **pálido**
pancakes **las crepes**
paper **el papel**; (newspaper) **el periódico**
paraffin **la parafina**
parcel **el paquete**
pardon? **¿cómo dice?**
parents **los padres**
park **el parque**; (verb) **aparcar**; no parking **prohibido aparcar**
parsley **el perejil**
parting (hair) **la raya**
party (celebration) **la fiesta**; (group) **el grupo**; (political) **el partido**
passenger **el pasajero**
passport **el pasaporte**
password **la contraseña**
pasta **la pasta**
path **el camino**
pavement **la acera**
pay **pagar**
payment **el pago**
peach **el melocotón**
peanuts **los cacahuetes**
pear **la pera**
pearl **la perla**
peas **los guisantes**
pedestrian **el peatón**
pedestrian zone **la zona peatonal**
peg **la pinza**

pen la pluma
pencil el lápiz
pencil sharpener el sacapuntas
penknife la navaja
pen pal el amigo/la amiga
  por correspondencia
people la gente
pepper la pimienta;
  (red, green) el pimiento
peppermints las pastillas
  de menta
per: per night por noche
perfect perfecto
perfume el perfume
perhaps quizás
perm la permanente
pet passport el pasaporte
  de animales
petrol la gasolina
petrol station la gasolinera
pets los animales
  de compañía; los
  animales domésticos
phone book la guía telefónica
phone booth la cabina
  telefónica
phonecard la tarjeta telefónica
photocopier la fotocopiadora
photograph la foto (grafía);
  (verb) fotografiar
photographer el fotógrafo
phrase book el libro de frases
piano el piano
pickpocket el carterista
picnic el picnic
piece el pedazo
pill la pastilla
pillow la almohada
pilot el piloto
PIN el pin
pin el alfiler
pine (tree) el pino
pineapple la piña
pink rosa
pipe (for smoking) la pipa;
  (for water) la tubería
piston el piston
pitch la plaza
pizza la pizza
place el lugar; *at your place*
  en su casa
plant la planta
plaster la tirita
plastic el plástico
plastic bag la bolsa de plástico
plastic wrap el plástico
  para envolver
plate el plato
platform (train) el andén
play (theatre) la obra
  de teatro; (verb) jugar

please por favor
pleased to meet you
  encantado/encantada
plug (electrical) el enchufe;
  (sink) el tapón
plumber el fontanero/
  la fontenera
pocket el bolsillo
poison el veneno
police la policía
police officer el policía
police report la denuncia
police station la comisaría
politics la política
poor pobre; (bad quality)
  malo
pop music la música pop
pork la carne de cerdo
port (harbour) el puerto;
  (drink) el oporto
porter (hotel) el conserje
Portugal Portugal
Portuguese portugués
possible posible
post el correo; (verb) echar
  al correo
postbox el buzón
postcard la postal
postcode el código postal
poster el póster
postman el cartero
post office (la oficina de)
  Correos
potato la patata
poultry las aves
pound (sterling) la libra
powder el polvo;
  (cosmetic) los polvos
pram el cochecito
prawns las gambas
prefer preferir
pregnant embarazada
prescription la receta
pretty bonito; (quite) bastante
price el precio
priest el cura
printer la impresora
private privado
problem el problema
profession la profesión
professor el catedrático
profits los beneficios
prohibited prohibido
protection factor (SPF) el
  factor de protección
public público
public holiday el día de
  fiesta
public swimming pool
  la piscina municipal
pull tirar de

puncture el pinchazo
purple morado
purse la cartera,
  el monedero
push empujar
pushchair la sillita de ruedas
put poner
pyjamas el pijama
Pyrenees los Pirineos

Q

quality la calidad
quarter el cuarto
question la pregunta
quick rápido
quiet tranquilo;
  (person) callado
quite (fairly) bastante;
  (fully) completamente

R

rabbit el conejo
radiator el radiador
radio la radio
radish el rábano
rake el rastrillo
railway el ferrocarril
rain la lluvia
raincoat la gabardina
rainforest la selva
raisins las pasas
raspberry la frambuesa
rare (uncommon) raro;
  (steak) poco hecho,
  poco pasado
rat la rata
razor blades
  las cuchillas de afeitar
read leer
ready listo
ready meals
  los platos preparados
receipt el recibo
reception la recepción
receptionist el/
  la recepcionista
record (music) el disco;
  (sport etc) el récord
record player el tocadiscos
record store la tienda de discos
red rojo; (wine) tinto
refreshments los refrescos
refrigerator el frigorífico
registered post
  correo certificado
relative el pariente
relax relajarse; (rest)
  descansar
religion la religión

remember: I remember
me acuerdo; I don't
remember no me acuerdo
repair arreglar
report el informe
reservation la reserva
rest (remainder) el resto;
(verb: relax) descansar
restaurant el restaurante
restaurant car
el vagón-restaurante
return (come back) volver;
(give back) devolver
return ticket el billete
de ida y vuelta
rice el arroz
rich rico
right (correct) correcto;
(not left) derecho
ring (for finger) el anillo
ripe maduro
river el río
road la carretera
roasted asado
robbery el robo
rock (stone) la roca
roll (bread) el bollo
roof el tejado
room la habitación; (space)
el sitio
room service el servicio
de habitaciones
rope la cuerda
rose la rosa
round (circular) redondo
roundabout la rotonda
row (verb) remar
rowing boat la barca de remos
rubber (material) la goma
rubber band la goma
rubbish la basura
ruby (stone) el rubí
rug (mat) la alfombra;
(blanket) la manta
rugby el rugby
ruins las ruinas
ruler (for measuring) la regla
rum el ron
run (verb) correr
runway la pista

S

sad triste
safe (not dangerous)
seguro
safety pin el imperdible
sailboard la tabla
de windsurfing
sailing la vela
salad la ensalada

sale (at reduced prices)
las rebajas
sales las ventas
salmon el salmón
salt la sal
same: the same dress el
mismo vestido; the same
people la misma gente;
same again, please lo
mismo otra vez, por favor
sand la arena
sandals las sandalias
sand dunes las dunas
sandwich el bocadillo
sanitary towels las compresas
Saturday sábado
sauce la salsa
saucepan el cazo
saucer el platillo
sauna la sauna
sausage la salchicha
say decir; what did you
say? ¿qué ha dicho?;
how do you say ...?
¿cómo se dice ...?
scampi las gambas
scarf la bufanda; (head)
el pañuelo
schedule el programa
school la escuela
science las ciencias
scissors las tijeras
Scotland Escocia
Scottish escocés/escocesa
screen la pantalla
screw el tornillo
screwdriver el destornillador
sea el mar
seafood los mariscos
seat el asiento
seat belt el cinturón
de seguridad
second el segundo
second class de segunda
see ver; I can't see no veo;
I see comprendo
self-employed (person) el
autónomo/la autónoma
sell vender
seminar el seminario
send mandar
separate (adj) distinto
separated separado
September septiembre
serious serio
seven siete
seventeen diecisiete
seventy setenta
several varios
sew coser
shampoo el champú

shave el afeitado;
to have a shave afeitarse
shaving foam la espuma
de afeitar
shawl el chal
she ella
sheet la sábana; (of paper)
la hoja
shell la concha
shellfish mariscos
sherry el jerez
ship el barco
shirt la camisa
shoelaces los cordones
de los zapatos
shoe polish la crema
de zapatos
shoes los zapatos
shoe shop la zapatería
shop la tienda
shopping la compra; to go
shopping ir de compras
short corto; (height) bajo
shorts los pantalones cortos
shoulder el hombro
shower (bath) la ducha;
(rain) el chaparrón
shower gel el gel de ducha
shrimp las quisquillas
shutter (camera)
el obturador; (window)
el postigo
sick: I feel sick tengo náuseas;
to be sick (vomit) devolver
side (edge) el borde
side lights las luces
de posición
sights: the sights of ... los
lugares de interés de ...
sightseeing el turismo
silk la seda
silver (metal) la plata;
(colour) plateado
simple sencillo
sing cantar
single (ticket) de ida;
(only) único; (unmarried)
soltero/soltera
single room
la habitación individual
sink el fregadero
sister la hermana
six seis
sixteen dieciséis
sixty sesenta
skid patinar
skiing: to go skiing ir a esquiar
skin cleanser
la leche limpiadora
ski resort la estación
de esquí

skirt **la falda**
skis **los esquís**
sky **el cielo**
sleep **el sueño**; (verb) **dormir**
sleeper car **el coche-cama**
sleeping bag **el saco de dormir**
sleeping pill **el somnífero**
sleeve **la manga**
slip (underwear)
  la combinacíon
slippers **las zapatillas**
slow **lento**
small **pequeño**
smell **el olor**; (verb) **oler**
smile **la sonrisa**;
  (verb) **sonreír**
smoke **el humo**; (verb) **fumar**
snack **la comida ligera**
snow **la nieve**
so: so good **tan bueno**;
  not so much **no tanto**
soaking solution
  (for contact lenses)
  la solución limpiadora
soap **el jabón**
socks **los calcetines**
soda water **la soda**
sofa **el sofa**
soft **blando**
soil **la tierra**
somebody **alguien**
somehow **de algún modo**
something **algo**
sometimes **a veces**
somewhere **en alguna parte**
son **el hijo**
song **la canción**
sorry! **¡perdón!**; *I'm sorry*
  perdón/lo siento; *sorry?*
  (pardon) **¿cómo dice?**
soup **la sopa**
south **el sur**
South America **Sudamérica**
souvenir **el recuerdo**
spade **la pala**
spades (cards) **las picas**
Spain **España**
Spaniard **el español/**
  la española
speak **hablar**;
  do you speak ...? **¿habla ...?**;
  I don't speak ... **no hablo ...**
speed **la velocidad**
speed limit **el límite de**
  velocidad
spider **la araña**
spinach **las espinacas**
spoon **la cuchara**
sport **el deporte**
sports centre
  el centro deportivo

spring (mechanical) **el muelle**;
  (season) **la primavera**
square (in town) **la plaza**;
  (adj) **cuadrado**
staircase **la escalera**
stairs **las escaleras**
stamp **el sello**
stapler **la grapadora**
star **la estrella**
start (beginning) **el**
  principio; (verb)
  empezar
starters **los entrantes**
statement **la declaración**
station **la estación**
statue **la estatua**
steak **el filete**
steal **robar**; *it's been stolen*
  lo han robado
steamed **al vapor**
steamer (boat) **el vapor**
stepdaughter **la hijastra**
stepfather **el padastro**
stepmother **la madastra**
stepson **el hijastro**
still water **el agua sin gas**
stockings **las medias**
stomach **el estómago**
stomach-ache **el dolor**
  de estómago
stop (bus) **la parada**; (verb)
  parar; *stop!* **¡alto!**
storm **la tormenta**
strawberries **las fresas**
stream (small river) **el arroyo**
street **la calle**
string **la cuerda**
stroller **la sillita de ruedas**
strong **fuerte**
student **el/la estudiante**
stupid **estúpido**
suburbs **las afueras**
sugar **el azúcar**
suit (clothing) **el traje**;
  it suits you **te sienta bien**
suitcase **la maleta**
sun **el sol**
sunbathe **tomar el sol**
sunburn **la quemadura de sol**
Sunday **domingo**
sunglasses **las gafas de sol**
sunny: it's sunny **hace sol**
sunshade **la sombrilla**
sunstroke **la insolación**
suntan: to get a suntan
  broncearse
suntan lotion
  la loción bronceadora
suntanned **bronceado**
supermarket **el supermercado**
supper **la cena**

supplement **el suplemento**
suppository **el supositorio**
sure **seguro**
surname **el apellido**
sweat **el sudor**; (verb) **sudar**
sweater **el jersey**
sweatshirt **la sudadera**
sweet (adj: not sour) **dulce**;
  sweets **los caramelos** (m)
swim (verb) **nadar**
swimming **la natación**
swimming pool **la piscina**
swimming trunks **el bañador**
switch **el interruptor**
synagogue **la sinagoga**
syringe **la jeringuilla**
syrup **el jarabe**

T

table **la mesa**
tablet **la pastilla**
take **tomar**
take off **el despegue**
talcum powder
  los polvos de talco
talk **la charla**; (verb)
  hablar
tall **alto**
tampons **los tampones**
tangerine **la mandarina**
tap **el grifo**
tapestry **el tapiz**
taxi **el taxi**
taxi rank **la parada de** *taxis*
tea **el té**
teacher **el profesor/**
  la profesora
technician **el técnico**
telephone **el teléfono**; (verb)
  llamar por teléfono
television **la televisión**
temperature **la temperatura**;
  (fever) **la fiebre**
ten **diez**
tennis **el tenis**
tent **la tienda** (de campaña)
tent peg
  la estaquilla, la estaca
tent pole **el mástil**
terminal **la terminal**
terrace **la terraza**
test **la prueba**
than **que**
thank (verb) **agradecer**;
  thank you/thanks **gracias**;
that **ese/esa, eso**;
  that bus **ese autobús**;
  that man **ese hombre**;
  that woman **esa mujer**;
  what's that? **¿qué es eso?**;

I think that ... **creo que ...;**
that one **ése/ésa**
the **el/la;** (plural) **los/las**
theatre **el teatro**
their: their room **su**
habitación; *their books* **sus libros;** *it's theirs* **es suyo**
them: it's for them **es para ellos/ellas;**
give it to them **déselo**
then **entonces;** (after) **después**
there **allí;** *there is/are ...* **hay ...;** *is/are there ...?* **¿hay ...?**
these: these men **estos hombres;** *these women* **estas mujeres;** *these are mine* **éstos son míos**
they **ellos/ellas**
thick **grueso**
thief **el ladrón**
thin **delgado**
think **pensar;**
I think so **creo que sí;**
I'll think about it **lo pensaré**
third **tercero**
thirsty: I'm thirsty **tengo sed**
thirteen **trece**
thirty **treinta**
this: this one **éste/ésta;**
this man **este hombre;**
this woman **esta mujer;**
what's this? **¿qué es esto?;**
this is Mr ... **éste es el señor ...**
those: those men **esos hombres;** *those women* **esas mujeres**
thousand **mil**
throat **la garganta**
through **por**
three **tres**
thunderstorm **la tormenta**
Thursday **jueves**
ticket (train etc) **el billete;** (theatre etc) **la entrada**
ticket office **la taquilla**
tide **la marea**
tie **la corbata;** (verb) **atar**
tight **ajustado**
tights **las medias, los pantis**
time **tiempo;** *what's the time?* **¿qué hora es?**
timetable **el horario**
tin **la hojalata**
tip (end) **la punta;** (money) **la propina**
tired **cansado**
tissues **los pañuelos de papel**
to: to America **a América;** *to the station* **a la estación;** *to*

the doctor **al médico**
toast **la tostada**
tobacco **el tabaco**
tobacconist **el estanco**
today **hoy**
together **juntos**
toilet (room in house) **el baño;** (bathroom item) **el váter;** (in public establishment) **los servicos**
toilet paper **el papel higiénico**
toilets (men) **los servicios de caballeros;** (women) **los servicios de señoras**
tomato **el tomate**
tomato juice **el zumo de tomate**
tomorrow **mañana**
tongue **la lengua**
tonic **la tónica**
tonight **esta noche**
too (also) **también;** (excessively) **demasiado**
tooth **el diente;**
back tooth **la muela**
toothache **el dolor de muelas**
toothbrush **el cepillo de dientes**
toothpaste **la pasta dentífrica**
torch **la linterna**
tour **la excursión**
tourist **el/la turista**
tourist office **la oficina de turismo**
towel **la toalla**
tower **la torre**
town **el pueblo**
town hall **el ayuntamiento**
toy **el juguete**
trade fair **la feria**
track suit **el chandal**
tractor **el tractor**
tradition **la tradición**
traffic **el tráfico**
traffic jam **el atasco**
traffic lights **el semáforo**
trailer **la caravana, el remolque**
train **el tren**
trainee **el aprendiz**
trainers **los zapatos de deporte**
translate **traducir**
translator **el traductor/ la traductora**
travel agency **la agencia de viajes**
tray **la bandeja**
tree **el árbol**
trolley **el carrito**

trousers **el pantalón**
truck **el camión**
true **cierto;** *it's true* **es verdad**
try **intentar**
Tuesday **martes**
tunnel **el túnel**
turn (left/right) **tuerza** (a la izquierda/ a la derecha)
turn: it's my turn **me toca a mí**
tweezers **las pinzas**
twelve **doce**
twenty **veinte**
two **dos**
typewriter **la máquina de escribir**
tyre **el neumático**

U

ugly **feo**
umbrella **el paraguas**
uncle **el tío**
under ... **debajo de ...**
underground (railway) **el metro**
underpants **los calzoncillos**
understand **entender;**
I don't understand **no entiendo**
underwear **la ropa interior**
United States **Estados Unidos**
university **la universidad**
unleaded **sin plomo**
until **hasta**
unusual **poco común**
up **arriba;** (upward) **hacia arriba**
urgent **urgente**
us: it's for us **es para nosotros/nosotras;**
give it to us **dénoslo**
use **el uso;** (verb) **usar;** *it's no use* **no sirve de nada**
useful **útil**
usual **corriente**
usually **en general**

V

vacancies (rooms) **habitaciones libres**
vaccination **la vacuna**
vacuum cleaner **la aspiradora**
valley **el valle**
valve **la válvula**
vanilla **la vainilla**
vase **el jarrón**
veal **la** (carne de) **ternera**

vegetables **la verdura**
vegetarian **vegetariano**
vehicle **el vehículo**
very **muy**; very much **mucho**
vest **la camiseta**
vet **el veterinario**
video (tape) **la cinta de vídeo**; (film) **el vídeo**
video games **los vídeo-juegos**
video recorder **el (aparato de) vídeo**
view **la vista**
viewfinder **el visor de imagen**
villa **el chalet**
village **el pueblo**
vinegar **el vinagre**
violin **el violín**
visit **la visita; visitar** (verb)
visiting hours **las horas de visita**
visitor **el/la visitante**
vitamin pills **las vitaminas**
vodka **el vodka**
voice **la voz**
voicemail **la mensajería de voz**

W

wait **esperar**; wait! **¡espere!**
waiter **el camarero**; waiter! **¡camarero!**
waiting room **la sala de espera**
waitress **la camarera**; waitress! **¡Oiga, por favor!**
Wales **Gales**
walk (stroll) **el paseo**; (verb) **andar**; to go for a walk **ir de paseo**
wall **la pared**; (outside) **el muro**
wallet **la cartera**
want (verb) **querer**
war **la guerra**
wardrobe **el armario**
warm **caliente**; (weather) **caluroso**
was **estaba/era**
washing machine **la zapatilla**
washing powder **el jabón de lavadora, el detergente**
washing-up liquid **el lavavajillas**
wasp **la avispa**
watch **el reloj**; (verb) **mirar**
water **el agua**
waterfall **la cascada**
water heater **el calentador** (de agua)

wave **la ola**; (verb) **agitar**
wavy (hair) **ondulado**
we **nosotros/nosotras**
weather **el tiempo**
website **la web site, el sitio web**
wedding **la boda**
Wednesday **miércoles**
weeds **las malas hierbas**
week **la semana**
welcome (adj) **bienvenido**; (verb) **dar la bienvenida**; you're welcome **no hay de qué**
wellington boots **las botas de agua**
Welsh **galés/galesa**
were: you were (informal singular) **eras/estabas**; (formal singular) **era/estaba**; (informal plural) **erais/estabais**; (formal plural) **eran/estaban**; we were **éramos/estábamos**; they were **eran/estaban**
west **el oeste**
wet **mojado**
what? **¿qué?**
wheel **la rueda**
wheel brace **la llave de las tuercas**
wheelchair **la silla de ruedas**
when? **¿cuándo?**
where? **¿dónde?**
whether **si**
which? **¿cuál?**
whisky **el whisky**
white **blanco**
white coffee **el café con leche**
who? **¿quién?**
why? **¿por qué?**
wide **ancho**; 3 metres wide **de tres metros de anchura**
wife **la mujer**
wind **el viento**
window **la ventana**
windscreen **el parabrisas**
wine **el vino**
wine list **la carta de vinos**
wine merchant **el vinatero**
wing **el ala**
with **con**
without **sin**
witness **el testigo**
woman **la mujer**
wood (material) **la madera**
wool **la lana**
word **la palabra**

work **el trabajo**; (verb) **trabajar**; (to function) **funcionar**
worktop **el mostrador**
worse **peor**
worst (el) **peor**
wrapping paper **el papel de envolver**; (for presents) **el papel de regalo**
wrench **la llave inglesa**
wrist **la muñeca**
writing paper **el papel de escribir**
wrong **equivocado**

X, Y, Z

x-ray department **el servicio de radiología**
year **el año**
yellow **amarillo**
yes **sí**
yesterday **ayer**
yet **todavía**; not yet **todavía no**
yoghurt **el yogur**
you (informal singular) **tú**; (formal singular) **usted**; (informal plural, m/f) **vosotros/ vosotras**; (formal plural) **ustedes**
young **joven**
your: your book (informal singular) **tu libro**; (formal singular) **su libro**; your shoes (informal singular) **tus zapatos**; (formal singular) **sus zapato**
yours: is this yours? (informal) **¿es tuyo esto?**; (formal) **¿es suyo esto?**
youth hostel **el albergue juvenil**
zip **la cremallera**
zoo **el zoo**

DICTIONARY
Spanish to English

The gender of Spanish nouns listed here is indicated by the abbreviations (m) for masculine nouns and (f) for feminine nouns. Plural nouns are followed by the abbreviations (m pl) or (f pl). Spanish adjectives (adj) vary according to the gender and number of the word they describe, and the masculine form is shown here. In general, adjectives that end in **-o** adopt an **-a** ending in the feminine form, and those that end in **-e** usually stay the same. For the plural form, **-s** is added.

A

a to; **a América** to America; **a la estación** to the station; **al médico** to the doctor; **a las tres** at 3 o'clock

abanico (m) fan (handheld)

abierto open (adj)

abogado/abogada (m/f) lawyer

abrebotellas (m) bottle opener

abrelatas (m) can opener

abrigo (m) coat

abril April

abrir to open

abuela (f) grandmother

abuelo (m) grandfather

abuelos (m pl) grandparents

aburrido boring

acaba de llegar it's just arrived

accidente (m) accident

aceite (m) oil; **el aceite de oliva** olive oil

aceituna (f) olive

acelerador (m) accelerator

acera (f) pavement

acondicionador (m) conditioner (hair)

acuerdo: me acuerdo I remember; **no me acuerdo** I don't remember

adaptador (m) adaptor

adelantar overtake (car)

adiós goodbye

aduana (f) customs

aerodeslizador (m) hovercraft

aeropuerto (m) airport

afeitado (m) shave; **afeitarse** to have a shave

after-shave (m) aftershave

afueras (f pl) suburbs

agencia (f) agency

agencia de viajes (f) travel agency

agenda (f) diary

agitar to wave

agosto August

agradable pleasant

agradecer to thank

agua (m) water; **el agua con gas** fizzy water; **el agua mineral** mineral water; **el agua potable** drinking water; **el agua sin gas** still water

aguja (f) needle

ahora now; **¿y ahora qué?** what next?

aire (m) air

aire acondicionado (m) air conditioning

ajedrez (m) chess

ajo (m) garlic

ajustado tight

ala (m) wing

albañil (m) builder

albaricoque (m) apricot

albergue juvenil (m) youth hostel

alcachofa (f) artichoke

alcohol (m) alcohol

alegre glad

alemán German

Alemania Germany

alérgico allergic

alfiler (m) pin

alfombra (f) carpet; rug

algo something

algodón (m) cotton, cotton wool

alguien somebody

alguna: en alguna parte somewhere

allí there, over there

almohada (f) pillow

alojamiento (m) accommodation

alquilar to hire

alto high, tall, loud

¡alto! stop!

amante (m/f) lover

amargo bitter

amarillo yellow

ambulancia (f) ambulance

América America

americano/americana (m/f) American

amigo/amiga (m/f) friend; **amigo/amiga por correspondencia** (m/f) pen pal

amontillado medium (sherry)

amor (m) love

ampliación (f) enlargement

ampolla (f) blister

análisis de sangre (m) blood test

andar to walk

andén (m) platform

anfiteatro (m) lecture theatre

anfitriona (f) hostess

anillo (m) ring (jewellery)

animal (m) animal; **los animales de compañía/los animales domésticos** pets

año (m) year

antes de ... before ...

anticonceptivo (m) contraceptive

anticongelante (m) antifreeze

anticuario (m) antique shop

antiséptico (m) antiseptic

aparcamiento (m) car park

aparcar to park; **prohibido aparcar** no parking

apartamento (m) apartment

apellido (m) surname

aperitivo (m) aperitif

apetito (m) appetite

aprender learn

aprendiz (m) *trainee*
apretón de manos (m)
   handshake
araña (f) *spider*
árbol (m) *tree*
árbol de levas (m) *camshaft*
arcón (m) *chest* (furniture)
arena (f) *sand*
Argelia *Algeria*
armario (m) *cupboard,*
   wardrobe
arreglar *repair*
arriba *up;* **hacia arriba**
   upward
arroyo (m) *stream* (small river)
arroz (m) *rice*
arte (m) *art*
artículos de punto
   (m pl) *knitwear*
artista (m/f) *artist*
asado *roasted*
ascensor (m) *lift*
asiento (m) *seat;*
   el asiento infantil
   car seat (for a baby/child)
asistenta (f) *cleaner*
asmático *asthmatic*
aspiradora (f) *vacuum*
   cleaner
aspirina (f) *aspirin*
atar *to tie*
atasco (m) *traffic jam*
aterrizar *to land*
ático (m) *attic*
atractivo *attractive* (offer)
audífono (m) *hearing aid*
auriculares (m pl)
   headphones
Australia *Australia*
australiano/australiana
   (m/f) *Australian*
autobús (m) *bus;*
autobús del aeropuerto
   airport bus
autocaravana (f) *camper van*
automático *automatic*
autónomo/autónoma
   (m/f) *self-employed*
autopista (f) *motorway*
avería (f) (car) *breakdown;*
   he tenido una avería
   I've had a breakdown
aves (f pl) *poultry*
avión (m) *aircraft*
avispa (f) *wasp*
ayer *yesterday*
ayuda (f) *help*
ayudar *to help*
ayuntamiento (m) *town hall*
azúcar (m) *sugar*
azul *blue*

B

bacon (m) *bacon*
bailar *to dance*
baile (m) *dance*
bajarse *to get off* (bus
   etc) ; *to get out*
bajo *low, short*
balandro (m) *sailing boat*
balcón (m) *balcony*
Baleares: las (Islas)
   Baleares *Balearic Islands*
balón (m) *football (ball);*
   el balón de playa
   beach ball
baloncesto (m) *basketball*
bañador (m) *bathing*
   suit, swimming trunks
banco (m) *bank*
banda (f) *band* (musicians)
bandeja (f) *tray*
bandera (f) *flag*
baño (m) *bath, bathroom, toilet*
   (room in a house); **darse un**
   baño *to have a bath;* **el traje**
   de baño *bathing suit*
bar (m) *bar* (drinks)
baraja (f) *deck of cards*
barato *inexpensive*
barba (f) *beard*
barbacoa (f) *barbecue*
barca (f) *small boat;*
   la barca de remos
   rowing boat
barco (m) *boat, ship*
barra de labios (f)
   lipstick
bastante *enough,*
   quite, fairly
basura (f) *litter, rubbish*
batería (f) *battery* (car)
bebé (m) *baby*
beber *to drink;* **¿quiere**
   beber algo? *would*
   you like something
   to drink?
bebida (f) *drink*
beige *beige*
beneficios (m pl) *profits*
berenjenas (f pl) *aubergines*
biblioteca (f) *library*
bicicleta (f) *bicycle;* **la**
   bicicleta de montaña
   mountain bike
bien *good;* **te sienta bien**
   it suits you
bienvenido *welcome*
bigote (m) *moustache*
billete (m) *fare, ticket* (train
   etc); **billete de ida y**
   vuelta (m) *return ticket*

billete de banco (m)
   banknote
bizcocho (m) *sponge cake*
blanco *white*
blando *soft*
bloc (m) *notepad*
bloque de oficinas (m)
   office block
blusa (f) *blouse*
boca (f) *mouth*
bocadillo (m) *sandwich*
boda (f) *wedding*
bodega (f) *cellar*
bolígrafo (m) *ballpoint pen*
bollo (m) *roll* (bread)
bolsa (f) *bag, packet* (sweets,
   crisps); l**a bolsa de basura**
   bin liner; **la bolsa de**
   plástico *plastic bag*
bolsillo (m) *pocket*
bolso (m) *handbag*
bombilla (f) *light bulb*
bonito *nice, pretty,*
   attractive (object)
bordado (m) *embroidery*
borde (m) *edge, border, side*
borracho *drunk*
bosque (m) *forest*
bota (f) *boot*
botas de agua (f pl)
   wellington boots
botella (f) *bottle*
botón (m) *button*
brazo (m) *arm*
bridge (m) *bridge* (game)
británico/británica
   (m/f) *British*
brocha (f) *paint brush*
broche (m) *brooch*
broma (f) *joke*
bronceado *suntanned*
broncearse *suntan: to get*
   a suntan
buenas noches *good evening*
buenas tardes *good*
   afternoon
bueno *good, good to eat, tasty*
buenos días *good morning*
bufanda (f) *scarf*
buzón (m) *postbox*

C

cabeza (f) *head*
cabina telefónica (f) *phone*
   booth
cable alargador (m)
   extension cord
cacahuetes (m pl) *peanuts*
cada *every, each;* **viente euros**
   cada uno *20 euros each*

café (m) *café, coffee;*
el café con leche
white coffee; **el café**
instantáneo *instant coffee;*
el café solo *espresso*
caja (f) *box; check-out;* **la caja**
de bombones *box of*
chocolates; **la caja de**
cambios *gearbox*
cajero (m) *cashier;*
el cajero automático
ATM, cashpoint
cajetilla (f) *packet (cigarettes)*
calambre (m) *cramp*
calcetines (m pl) *socks*
calculadora (m) *calculator*
calefacción (f) *heating;*
la calefacción central
central heating
calentador (de agua) (m)
water heater
calidad (f) *quality*
caliente *warm*
callado *quiet (person)*
calle (f) *street;* **la calle**
principal *main road*
caluroso *warm (weather)*
calzoncillos (m pl) *underpants*
cama (f) *bed*
cámara de fotos (f) *camera*
cámara neumática (f)
inner tube
camarera (f) *waitress*
camarero (m) *waiter;*
¡camarero! *waiter!*
cambiar *to change (money)*
cambiarse *to change (clothes)*
cambio (m) *change (money);*
exchange rate
camino (m) *path*
camión (m) *truck*
camisa (f) *shirt*
camiseta (f) *vest*
camisón (m) *nightgown*
campana (f) *bell (church)*
camping (m) *campsite*
camping-gas (m) *camping gas*
campo (m) *countryside, field*
Canadá *Canada*
canadiense *Canadian*
canal (m) *canal*
Canarias: las (Islas)
Canarias Canaries
canción (f) *song*
candado (m) *padlock*
cangrejo (m) *crab*
cansado *tired*
cantar *to sing*
capazo (m) *crib*
capó (m) *bonnet (car)*
cara (f) *face*

caramelos (m) *sweets*
caravana (f) *trailer*
carburador (m) *carburetor*
cardenal (m) *bruise*
cargador (m) *charger*
carne (f) *meat*
carne de cerdo (f) *pork*
carne de vaca (f) *beef*
carnet de conducir (m)
driving licence
carnicería (f) *butcher's*
caro *expensive*
carpintero (m) *carpenter*
carretera (f) *road*
carrito (m) *trolley*
carta (f) *letter (mail); menu;* **la**
carta de vinos (f) *wine list*
cartera (f) *purse, briefcase,*
wallet
carterista (m) *pickpocket*
cartero (m) *postman*
casa (f) *house, home;*
en casa *at home*
casado *married*
cascada (f) *waterfall*
casi *almost*
cassette (f) *cassette*
castaño *brown (hair)*
castañuelas (f pl) *castanets*
castellano *Castilian*
Castilla *Castile*
castillo (m) *castle*
Cataluña *Catalonia*
catedral (f) *cathedral*
catedrático (m) *professor*
católico *Catholic (adj)*
catorce *fourteen*
cazo (m) *saucepan*
cebo (m) *bait*
cebolla (f) *onion*
ceja (f) *eyebrow*
cementerio (m) *cemetery*
cena (f) *dinner, supper,*
dinner party
cenicero (m) *ashtray*
centro (m) *centre; city centre;*
el centro deportivo *sports*
centre; **en el centro**
middle: in the middle
cepillar el pelo *to brush hair*
cepillo (m) *brush (for cleaning);*
el cepillo del pelo *hair*
brush; **el cepillo de**
dientes *toothbrush*
cerca *near, close;* (f) *fence*
cereza (f) *cherry*
cerilla (f) *match (light)*
cerrado *closed*
cerrar *to close*
cerrojo (m) *bolt (on door)*
certificado (m) *certificate*

cerveza (f) *beer*
césped (m) *lawn*
cesto (m) *basket*
chal (m) *shawl*
chalet (m) *villa*
champiñones (m pl)
mushrooms
champú (m) *shampoo*
chandal (m) *track suit*
chaparrón (m) *shower*
(rain)
chaqueta (f) *jacket*
charcutería (f) *delicatessen*
charla (f) *talk*
cheque (m) *cheque*
chica (f) *girl*
chicle (m) *chewing gum*
chico (m) *boy*
chimenea (f) *chimney,*
fireplace
chincheta (f) *drawing pin*
chiste (m) *joke (funny story)*
chocolate (m) *chocolate*
chuleta (f) *chop (food)*
chupa-chups (m) *lollipop*
ciclismo (m) *cycling*
ciclomotor (m) *moped*
ciego *blind (cannot see)*
cielo (m) *sky*
cien *hundred*
ciencias (f pl) *science*
cierto *true*
cigalas (f pl) *crayfish*
cigarrillo (m) *cigarette*
cinco *five*
cincuenta *fifty*
cine (m) *cinema*
cinta (f) *cassette;* **el cinta**
de vídeo *video tape*
cinturón (m) *belt;* **el cinturón**
de seguridad *seat belt*
cita (f) *appointment*
ciudad (f) *city, town;*
el centro ciudad *city*
centre
claro *clear (water); light*
(adj: not dark)
clase (f) *class; lesson*
clavo (m) *nail (metal)*
claxon (m) *horn (car)*
cliente (m) *client*
cobrador (m) *conductor (bus)*
cobrar *to cash*
cocer *to cook, boil*
cocer al horno *to bake*
coche (m) *car*
coche-cama (m) *sleeper car*
cochecito (m) *pram*
cocina (f) *cooker; kitchen*
cocinero/cocinera (m/f) *cook*
coctel (m) *cocktail party*

código code; **el código de la circulación** highway code; **el código postal** postcode
codo (m) elbow
coger catch; **coger el tren** to catch the train
cojín (m) cushion
col (f) cabbage
cola (f) line
colada (f) laundry (washed)
colcha (f) bedspread
colchón (m) mattress
colchoneta (f) air mattress
colección (f) collection (stamps etc)
coliflor (f) cauliflower
collar (m) collar (of animal)
collar (m) necklace; colour
combinación (f) slip (underwear)
comedor (m) dining room
comer to eat
comida (f) food, meal; lunch
comida ligera (f) snack
comisaría (f) police station
como like; **como éste** like this one
¿cómo? how?; **¿cómo se llama usted?** what's your name?**¿cómo dice?** pardon?, what did you say?
cómoda (f) chest of drawers
compañía aérea (f) airline
compartimento (m) compartment
completamente completely
complicado complicated
compra (f) shopping
comprar to buy
comprendo I see
compresas (f pl) sanitary towels
con with
coñac (m) brandy
concha (f) shell
concierto (m) concert
concurrido crowded
condón (m) condom
conducir to drive
conductor (m) driver
conejo (m) rabbit
conferencia (f) conference; **la sala de conferencias** conference room
congelador (m) freezer
congelados (m pl) frozen foods
conocer to know (person, place)
conserje (m) porter (hotel)
consulado (m) consulate
contable (m/f) accountant
contenedor de basura (m) bin
contento happy

contestador automático (m) answering machine
contra against
contraseña (f) password
contrato (m) contract
copa (f) glass (for drinking)
corazón (m) heart
corazones (m pl) hearts (cards)
corbata (f) tie
corcho (m) cork
cordero (m) lamb
cordones (de los zapatos) (m pl) (shoe)laces
correa (f) lead
correcto right (correct)
correo (m) mail, post; **el correo certificado** registered post; **el correo electrónico** email
Correos: (la oficina de) **Correos** (f) post office
correr to run
corrida de toros (f) bullfight
corriente ordinary; usual
cortadura (f) cut
cortar to chop, cut
cortauñas (m) nail clippers
corte de pelo (m) haircut
cortina (f) curtain
corto short
coser to sew
cosméticos (m pl) cosmetics
costar to cost; **¿cuánto cuesta?** what does it cost?
crema (f) cream (lotion)
crema de zapatos (f) shoe polish
cremallera (f) zip
creo que ... I think that ...
crepes (f pl) pancakes
crisis nerviosa (f) nervous breakdown
cristal (m) glass (material)
crucero (m) cruise
cuaderno (m) notebook
cuadrado square (adj)
¿cuál? which?
cualquiera de ellos either of them
¿cuándo? when?
¿cuánto cuesta? what does it cost?, how much is it?
¿cuántos años tiene? how old are you?
cuarenta forty
cuarto (m) quarter, room; (adj) fourth
cuarto de baño (m) bathroom
cuarto de estar (m) living room, lounge
cuatro four

cubo (m) bucket; **el cubo de la basura** dustbin
cucaracha (f) cockroach
cuchara (f) spoon
cuchillas de afeitar (f pl) razor blades
cuchillo (m) knife
cuello (m) neck, collar
cuenco (m) bowl
cuenta (f) bill
cuerda (f) string; rope
cuerno (m) horn (animal)
cuero (m) leather
cuerpo (m) body
cueva (f) cave
¡cuidado! be careful!
cumpleaños (m) birthday
cuna (f) cot
cura (m) priest
curry (m) curry

D

dar give; **dar la bienvenida** to welcome
de of; **de algún modo** somehow; **de ida** single (ticket)
debajo de below, under
decir say; **¿qué ha dicho?** what did you say?; **¿cómo se dice ...?** how do you say ...?
declaración (f) statement
dedo (m) finger
delante de in front of ...
delgado thin
demasiado too (excessively)
démelo give it to me
dentadura postiza (f) dentures, false teeth
dentista (m/f) dentist
denuncia (f) police report
departamento (m) department
deporte (m) sport
derecho (m) law, justice; **no hay derecho** it's not fair; (adj) right (not left)
desayuno (m) breakfast
descansar to rest
descuento (m) discount
desmayarse to faint
desodorante (m) deodorant
despacho (m) office (room)
despegue (m) take off
despertador (m) alarm clock
después then (after); **después de ...** after ...
destornillador (m) screwdriver
detergente (m) washing powder
detrás de ... behind ...
devolver to return (give back); to be sick (vomit)

día (m) *day;* **el día de fiesta** *public holiday*
diabético *diabetic*
diamantes (m pl) *diamonds*
diarrea (f) *diarrhoea*
diccionario (m) *dictionary*
diciembre *December*
diecinueve *nineteen*
dieciocho *eighteen*
dieciséis *sixteen*
diecisiete *seventeen*
diente (m) *tooth*
diesel *diesel* (adj: engine)
diez *ten*
diferente *different*
difícil *difficult*
dígame *hello* (on phone)
dinero (m) *money, cash;* **no tengo dinero** *I have no money*
dirección (f) *address*
director/directora (m/f) *manager* (hotel); *conductor* (orchestra)
disco (m) *record* (music)
disco compacto (m) *compact disc*
discoteca (f) *nightclub*
diseñador/diseñadora (m/f) *designer*
disponible *available*
distancia *distance;* **¿qué distancia hay a ...?** *how far is it to ...?*
distinto *separate, different* (adj); **¡eso es distinto!** *that's different!;* **quería otro distinto** *I'd like a different one*
diversiones (f pl) *entertainment*
divertido; (odd) **raro** *funny*
divorciado *divorced*
doce *twelve*
documento (m) *document*
dólar (m) *dollar*
dolor (m) *ache, pain;* **el dolor de cabeza** *headache;* **el dolor de estómago** *stomach-ache;* **el dolor de muelas** *toothache*
domingo *Sunday*
¿dónde? *where?;* **¿dónde está ...?** *where is ...?*
dónut (m) *doughnut*
dormir *to sleep*
dormitorio (m) *bedroom*
dos *two;* **los dos** *both*
ducha (f) *shower* (bath)
dulce *sweet* (adj: not sour)

dunas (f pl) *sand dunes*
durante *during*
duro *hard* (not soft)
duty-free (m) *duty-free shop*

E

echar al correo *to post*
echar el cerrojo *to bolt*
edificio (m) *building*
edredón (m) *duvet*
eje (m) *axle*
ejecutivo (m) *executive*
ejemplo (m) *example;* **por ejemplo** *for example*
él *he, him, the* (m); **es para él** *it's for him*
elástico *elastic*
electricidad (f) *electricity*
electricista (m/f) *electrician*
eléctrico *electric*
ella *she, her, the* (f); **es para ella** *it's for her*
ellos/ellas *they, them;* **es para ellos/ellas** *it's for them*
email (m) *email;* **la dirección de email** *email address*
embajada (f) *embassy*
embarazada *pregnant*
embarazoso *embarrassing*
emergencia (f) *emergency*
empaste (m) *filling* (in tooth)
empezar *to start*
empleado (m) *employee*
empujar *to push*
en *on, at, in;* **en inglés** *in English;* **en el hotel** *in the hotel;* **en Barcelona** *in Barcelona;* **en Correos** *at the post office;* **en su casa** *at your place*
encaje (m) *lace*
encantado/encantada (m/f) *pleased to meet you*
encargado (m) *caretaker*
encendedor (m) *lighter*
encendido (m) *ignition*
enchufe (m) *plug* (electrical)
encima de ... *over ...*
encuentro (m) *meeting;* **no me encuentro bien** *I don't feel well*
enero *January*
enfermo/enferma (m/f) *nurse*
enfrente de *opposite;* **enfrente del hotel** *opposite the hotel*
¡enhorabuena! *congratulations!*
ensalada (f) *salad*

entender *to understand;* **no entiendo** *I don't understand*
entonces *then, so*
entrada (f) *entrance, ticket* (theatre etc)
entrantes (m pl) *starters*
entre ... *between ...*
entrega (f) *delivery*
enviar por fax *to fax*
epiléptico *epileptic*
equipaje (m) *luggage;* **el equipaje de mano** *hand luggage*
equipo de música (m) *music system*
equivocación (f) *mistake*
equivocado *wrong*
era *you were* (formal): *it/he/she was*
éramos *we were*
eran *they were*
eras *you were* (informal)
eres *you are* (informal)
es *you are* (formal)
es *it/he/she is*
escalera (f) *staircase;* **la escalera mecánica** *escalator;* **las escaleras** *stairs*
escarcha (f) *frost*
escocés/escocesa (m/f) *Scottish*
Escocia *Scotland*
escopeta (f) *gun* (rifle)
escuela (f) *school*
ese/esa *that;* **ese autobús** *that bus;* **ese hombre** *that man;* **esa mujer** *that woman;* **¿qué es eso?** *what's that?*
ése/ésa *that, that one;*
esmalte de uñas (m) *nail polish*
esos/esas *those, those ones;* **esos hombres** *those men;* **esas mujeres** *those women*
espalda (f) *back* (body)
España *Spain*
español/española (m/f) *Spanish, Spaniard*
especialidad (f) *field of study*
espejo (m) *mirror*
esperar *to wait;* **¡espere!** *wait!*
espinacas (f pl) *spinach*
espuma de afeitar (f) *shaving foam*
espuma moldeadora (f) *mousse* (for hair)
esquina (f) *corner* (of street)

esquís (m pl) *skis*
está *you are* (formal)
está *it/he/she is*
esta noche *tonight*
estaba *it/he/she was; you were* (formal)
estábamos *we were*
estaban *they were*
estabas *you were* (informal)
estaca (f) *tent peg*
estación (f) *station;* **la estación de autobuses** *bus station;* **la estación de esquí** *ski resort;* **la estación de metro** *metro station*
Estados Unidos *United States*
estamos *we are*
están *they are*
estanco (m) *tobacconist*
estaquilla (f) *tent peg*
estás *you are* (informal)
estatua (f) *statue*
este *east;* **el Este** *the East*
éste/ésta *this, this one;* **este hombre** *this man;* **esta mujer** *this woman;* **¿qué es esto?** *what's this?;* **éste es el señor ...** *this is Mr ...*
estómago (m) *stomach*
estos/estas *these, these ones;* **estos hombres** *these men;* **estas mujeres** *these women;* **éstos son míos** *these are mine*
estoy *I am*
estrecho *narrow* (adj)
estrella (f) *star*
estudiante (m/f) *student*
estufa (f) *heater*
estúpido *stupid*
etiqueta (f) *label*
evidente *clear* (obvious)
excelente *excellent*
exceso de equipaje (m) *excess baggage*
excursión (f) *excursion, tour*
exposición (f) *exhibition*
externa *external*
extintor (m) *fire extinguisher*
extranjero/extranjera (m/f) *foreigner*

F

fácil *easy*
factor de protección (m) *protection factor* (SPF)
factura (f) *invoice*
facturación (f) *check-in*

facturar *to check in*
falda (f) *skirt*
falta: no hace falta *there's no need*
familia (f) *family*
fan (m) *fan* (enthusiast)
fantástico *fantastic*
farmacia (f) *chemist*
faros (m pl) *headlights*
febrero *February*
¡felicidades! *happy birthday!*
feliz *happy*
feo *ugly*
feria (f) *fair, trade fair*
ferretería (f) *hardware store*
ferrocarril (m) *railway*
ferry (m) *ferry*
fiebre (f) *temperature,* **fever;** **la fiebre del heno** *hay fever*
fiesta (f) *party* (celebration)
filete (m) *steak*
filtro (m) *filter*
fin (m) *end;* **¡por fin!** *at last!*
final (m) *end*
fino *dry* (sherry)
flash (m) *flash* (camera)
flauta (f) *flute*
flequillo (m) *fringe* (hair)
flexo (m) *angle-poise lamp*
flor (f) *flower*
folleto (m) *brochure, leaflet*
fonda (f) *inn*
fondo (m) *bottom*
fontanero/fontanera (m/f) *plumber*
foto (grafía) (f) *photograph*
fotocopiadora (f) *photocopier*
fotografiar *to photograph*
fotógrafo (m) *photographer*
fotómetro (m) *light meter*
frambuesa (f) *raspberry*
francés *French*
Francia *France*
fregadero (m) *sink*
freír *to fry*
frenar *to brake*
freno (m) *brake;* **el freno de emergencia** *emergency brake;* **el freno de mano** *handbrake*
fresas (f pl) *strawberries*
fresco *cool*
frigorífico (m) *fridge*
frío *cold* (adj); *I'm cold* **tengo frío**
frito *fried*
frontera (f) *border* (between countries)
fruta (f) *fruit*

fuego (m) *fire;* **los fuegos artificiales** *fireworks*
fuel-oil *diesel* (oil)
fuente (f) *fountain*
fuera *outside*
fuerte *strong*
fumar *to smoke*
funcionar *to work* (function)
fútbol (m) *football* (game)

G

gabardina (f) *raincoat*
gafas (f pl) *glasses;* **las gafas de sol** *sunglasses*
galería de arte (f) *art gallery*
Gales *Wales*
galés/galesa *Welsh*
galleta (f) *biscuit*
gambas (f pl) *prawns*
ganga (f) *bargain*
garage (m) *garage* (for parking)
garantía (f) *guarantee*
garantizar *to guarantee*
garganta (f) *throat*
gas para el encendedor (m) *lighter fuel*
gasolina (f) *petrol*
gasolinera (f) *petrol station*
gato (m) *cat*
gay *gay* (homosexual)
gel (m) *gel* (hair); **el gel de ducha** *shower gel*
gemelos (m pl) *cuff links*
general: en general *usually*
gente (f) *people*
gerente (m/f) *manager*
Gibraltar *Gibraltar*
ginebra (f) *gin*
gobierno (m) *government*
Golfo de Vizcaya (m) *Bay of Biscay*
goma (f) *rubber band; rubber* (material)
goma de borrar (f) *eraser*
gordo *fat* (adj)
gorra (f) *cap* (hat)
gorro (m) *woollen hat*
gotas (f pl) *drops*
gracias *thank you*
Gran Bretaña *Great Britain*
grande *big, large*
grandes almacenes (m pl) *department store*
granja (f) *farm*
granjero (m) *farmer*
grapadora (f) *stapler*
grasa (f) *fat* (meat etc)
gratis *free* (no charge)
grifo (m) *tap*

gris grey
gritar to shout
grosellas negras (f pl) blackcurrants
grueso thick
grupo (m) party (group)
guantes (m pl) gloves
guapo attractive, beautiful, handsome (person)
guerra (f) war
guía (m/f) guide; **la guía telefónica** phone book; **la guía turística** guide book
guisantes (m pl) peas
guisar to cook
guitarra (f) guitar
gustar like: **me gusta ...** I like ...; **me gusta nadar** I like swimming

H

habitación (f) room; **la habitación doble** double room; **la habitación individual** single room; **habitaciones libres** vacancies
hablar to talk; **¿habla ...?** do you speak ...?; **no hablo ...** I don't speak ...
hacer to do, make; **hacer auto-stop** to hitchhike; **hacer footing** to jog; **hacer punto** to knit; **hacer transbordo** to change (trains etc); **hace sol** it's sunny
hacha (m) axe
hacia abajo down
hambre hungry; **tengo hambre** I'm hungry
hamburguesa (f) hamburger
hámster (m) hamster
harina (f) flour
hasta until
hay... there is/are...; **¿hay ...?** is/are there ...?
helado (m) ice cream
hepatitis (f) hepatitis
herida (f) injury
hermana (f) sister
hermano (m) brother
hervido boiled
hervidor de agua (m) kettle
hervir to boil (water)
hidroaleta (f) hydrofoil
hielo (m) ice
hierba (f) grass
hierro (m) iron (material)
hígado (m) liver

higo (m) fig
hija (f) daughter
hijastra (f) stepdaughter
hijastro (m) stepson
hijo (m) son
hincha (m) football fan
historia (f) history
hobby (m) hobby
hoguera (f) campfire
hoja (f) leaf, sheet (of paper)
hojalata (f) tin
hola hello
hombre (m) man
hombro (m) shoulder
homeopatía (f) homeopathy
honrado honest
hora (f) hour; **¿qué hora es?** what's the time?
horario (m) timetable; **el horario de apertura** opening times
horca (f) garden fork
horno (m) oven
horrible awful, horrible
hospital (m) hospital
hoy today
hueso (m) bone
huevo (m) egg
húmedo damp
humo (m) smoke

I

idioma (m) language
iglesia (f) church
imperdible (m) safety pin
imposible impossible
impreso de solicitud (m) application form
impresora (f) printer
incendio (m) fire (blaze)
incluido included
indigestión indigestion
infección (f) infection
información (f) information
informe (m) report
ingeniería (f) engineering
Inglaterra England
inglés/inglesa English
inhalador (m) inhaler (for asthma etc)
inmediatamente immediately
insecto (m) insect
insolación (f) sunstroke
insomnio (m) insomnia
instrumento musical (m) musical instrument
intentar to try
interesante interesting
intermitente (m) indicator

internet (m) internet
interpretar to interpret
intérprete (m/f) interpreter
interruptor (m) switch
intoxicación alimenticia (f) food poisoning
invitación (f) invitation
invitada (f) guest
inyección (f) injection
ir to go; **ir a esquiar** to go skiing; **ir de compras** to go shopping
Irlanda Ireland; **Irlanda del Norte** Northern Ireland
irlandés/irlandesa Irish
isla (f) island
Italia Italy
italiano/italiana (m/f) Italian
izquierdo left (not right)

J

jabón (m) soap; **el jabón de lavadora** washing powder
jamón (m) ham
jarabe (m) syrup
jardín (m) garden
jarrita (f) mug
jarrón (m) vase
jaula (f) cage
jazz (m) jazz
jefe (m) manager
jengibre (m) ginger (spice)
jerez (m) sherry
jeringuilla (f) syringe
jersey (m) sweater
joven young
joyería (f) jeweller's
judías (f pl) beans
jueves Thursday
jugar to play
juguete (m) toy
julio July
junio June
junto a near; **junto a la puerta** near the door; **junto a la ventana** near the window
juntos together

K, L

kilo (m) kilo
kilómetro (m) kilometre
kiosko de periódicos (m) newsagent's
la (f) the
laca (f) hairspray
lado de (f) beside
ladrón (m) thief

lago (m) *lake*
lámpara (f) *lamp*
lamparilla de noche (f) *bedside lamp*
lana (f) *wool*
langosta (f) *lobster*
lápiz (m) *pencil*
largo *long*
las (f pl) *the*
lata (f) *can* (tin)
lavabo (m) *basin* (sink)
lavandería automática (f) *laundrette*
lavavajillas (m) *dishwasher*
laxante (m) *laxative*
leche (f) *milk*; **la leche limpiadora** *cleansing milk* (for skin)
lechuga (f) *lettuce*
leer *to read*
lejía *bleach*
lejos *far, far away*
lengua (f) *tongue*
lente (f) *lens*; **las lentes de contacto** *contact lenses*; **las lentes de contacto semi-rígidas** *gas-permeable lenses*
lento *slow*
letra (f) *letter* (of alphabet)
levantarse *to get up* (rise)
libra (f) *pound* (sterling)
libre *free* (not engaged)
libre de impuestos *duty-free*
libro (m) *book*; **el libro de frases** *phrase book*
licor (m) *liqueur*
ligero *light* (adj: not heavy)
lima (f) *lime* (fruit)
lima de uñas (f) *nailfile*
límite de velocidad (m) *speed limit*
limón (m) *lemon*
limonada (f) *lemonade*
limpio *clean* (adj)
línea (f) *line* (phone etc)
linterna (f) *torch*
lista (f) *list*
listo *clever; ready*
literatura (f) *literature*
litro (m) *litre*
llamar por teléfono *to telephone*
llave (f) *key*; **la llave de las tuercas** *wheel brace*; **la llave inglesa** *wrench*
llegar *to arrive*
lleno *crowded, full*; **estoy lleno** *I'm full* (up)
llorar *to cry* (weep)
lluvia (f) *rain*

lo/la *it*
lo antes posible *as soon as possible*
loción lotion (f); **la loción anti-mosquitos** *insect repellent lotion*; **la loción bronceadora** *suntan lotion*
loco *mad*
lona impermeable (f) *groundsheet*
longitud (f) *length*
los (m pl) *the*
lo siento *I'm sorry*
luces de posición (f pl) *side lights*
lugar (m) *place, sight*; **los lugares de interés de ...** *the sights of ...*
luna (f) *moon*
lunes *Monday*
luz (f) *light*

M

madastra (f) *stepmother*
madera (f) *wood* (material)
madre (f) *mother*
maduro *ripe*
malas hierbas (f pl) *weeds*
maleta (f) *suitcase*
maletero (m) *boot* (car)
Mallorca *Majorca*
malo *bad, poor* (quality)
mama *Mum*
mañana *tomorrow*
mañana (f) *morning*; **por la mañana** *in the morning*
mandar *to send*
mandarina (f) *tangerine*
manga (f) *sleeve*
mano (f) *hand*
manta (f) *blanket, rug*
mantequilla (f) *butter*
manzana (f) *apple*
mapa (m) *map*
maquillaje (m) *make-up*
maquina cortacésped (f) *lawn mower*
máquina de escribir (f) *typewriter*
máquina de fotos (f) *camera*
mar (m) *sea*
marea (f) *tide*
mareado *faint, dizzy*
margarina (f) *margarine*
marido (m) *husband*
mariscos (m pl) *seafood, shellfish*
mármol (m) *marble*
marrón *brown*
Marruecos *Morocco*

martes *Tuesday*
martillo (m) *hammer*
marzo *March*
más *more*; **más de ...** *more than ...*; **más tarde** *later*; **algo más** *something else*; **alguien más** *someone else*
mástil (m) *tent pole*
matrícula (f) *number plate*
mayo *may*
mecánico (m) *mechanic*
media pensión *half board*
medianoche *midnight*
medias (f pl) *tights, stockings*
medicina (f) *medicine*
médico/médica (m/f) *doctor*
medio *half*; **media hora** *half an hour*
mediodía (m) *midday, noon*
Mediterráneo: el Mediterráneo *Mediterranean*
medusa (f) *jellyfish*
mejillones (m pl) *mussels*
mejor *best/better*
melocotón (m) *peach*
melón (m) *melon*
menos *less*
mensaje (m) *message*
mensajería de voz (f) *voicemail*
menú (del día) (m) *set menu*
menudo: a menudo *often*
mercado (m) *market*
mermelada (f) *jam*; **la mermelada de naranja** *marmalade*
mes (m) *month*
mesa (f) *table*; **la mesa de escritorio** *desk*
mesilla de noche (f) *bedside table*
metro (m) *underground* (railway)
mi (s) *my*; **mi libro** *my book*; **mis llaves** *my keys*
microondas (m) *microwave*
miel (f) *honey*
miércoles *Wednesday*
mil *thousand*
minusválido *disabled*
minuto (m) *minute*
mío *mine*; **es mío** *it's mine*
mirar *to watch*
misa (f) *mass* (church)
mismo *same*; **el mismo vestido** *the same dress*; **la misma gente** *the same people*; **lo mismo otra vez, por favor** *same again, please*

mochila (f) *backpack*
moda (f) *fashion*
modem (m) *modem*
mojado *wet*
moneda (f) *coin*
monedero (m) *purse*
monitor (m) *monitor*
montaña (f) *mountain*
monte (m) *hill*
monumento (m) *monument*
morado *purple*
moras (f pl) *blackberries*
mordedura (f) *bite (dog)*
morder *to bite (dog)*
morir *to die*
mosaico (m) *mosaic*
mosca (f) *fly (insect)*
mosquito (m) *mosquito*
mostaza (f) *mustard*
mostrador (m) *worktop;* **el mostrador de facturación** *check-in desk*
motocicleta (f) *motorcycle*
motor (m) *engine (motor)*
motora (f) *motorboat*
mover *to move (something);* **moverse** *move oneself;* **¡no se mueva!** *don't move!*
mucho *much/many, a lot;* **mucho mejor** *much better;* **mucho más despacio** *much slower;* **no muchos** *not many*
mudarse *(de casa) to move (house)*
muebles (m pl) *furniture*
muela (f) *back tooth*
muelle (m) *dock; spring (mechanical)*
muerto *dead*
mujer (f) *woman, wife*
muletas (f pl) *crutches*
muñeca (f) *wrist*
muro (m) *wall (outside)*
museo (m) *museum*
música (f) *music;* **la música clásica** *classical music;* **la música folklórica** *folk music;* **la música pop** *pop music*
músico (m) *musician*
muy *very*

N

nací en … *I was born in …*
nada *nothing;* **no queda nada** *there's nothing left;* **no sirve de nada** *it's no use*
nadar *to swim*

nadie *nobody*
naranja (f) *orange (fruit);* *orange (adj)*
nariz (f) *nose*
nata (f) *cream (dairy)*
natación (f) *swimming*
náuseas *sick;* **tengo náuseas** *I feel sick*
navaja (f) *penknife*
navidad (f) *Christmas*
necesario *necessary*
necesito … *I need …*
negar *to deny*
negativo (m) *negative (photo)*
negocio (m) *business*
negro *black*
neozelandés/ neozelandesa *New Zealander*
neumático (m) *tyre*
ni … ni … *neither … nor …*
niebla (f) *fog*
nieta (f) *granddaughter*
nieto (m) *grandson*
nieve (f) *snow*
ninguno/ninguna: **ninguno de ellos** *neither of them;* **en ninguna parte** *nowhere*
niño/niña *child (m/f);* **los niños** *children;* **el niño pequeño** *baby*
no *no (response), not;* **no hay de qué** *you're welcome;* **no importa** *it doesn't matter;* **no es/está …** *(s) he's not …*
noche (f) *night*
nombre (m) *name;* **el nombre de pila** *first name*
norte (m) *north*
nosotros/nosotras *we, us;* **es para nosotros/ nosotras** *it's for us*
noticias (f pl) *news*
novela (f) *novel*
noventa *ninety*
novia (f) *girlfriend*
noviembre *November*
novio (m) *boyfriend*
nudista (m/f) *nudist*
nuestro *our;* **es nuestro** *it's ours*
Nueva Zelanda *New Zealand*
nueve *nine*
nuevo *new*
nuez (f) *nut (fruit)*
número (m) *number;* **los números** *figures*
nunca *never*

O

o *or;* **o bien … o …** *either … or …*
obra de teatro (f) *play (theatre)*
obturador (m) *shutter (camera)*
Océano Atlántico (m) *Atlantic Ocean*
ochenta *eighty*
ocho *eight*
octubre *October*
oculista (m/f) *optician*
ocupado *busy (engaged); occupied*
oeste (m) *west*
oficina (f) *office (place); branch (of company);* **la oficina de objetos perdidos** *lost property office;* **la oficina de turismo** *tourist office*
oído (m) *(inner) ear*
¡oiga, por favor! *excuse me! (to get attention); waiter/waitress!*
oír *to hear*
ojo (m) *eye*
ola (f) *wave*
oler *to smell*
olivo (m) *olive tree*
olor (m) *smell*
oloroso *sweet (sherry)*
olvidar *to forget*
once *eleven*
ondulado *wavy (hair)*
operación (f) *operation*
operadora (f) *operator*
oporto (m) *port (drink)*
orden del día (m) *agenda*
ordenador (m) *computer*
oreja *ear (f)*
órgano (m) *organ (music)*
oro (m) *gold*
orquesta (f) *orchestra*
oscuro *dark;* **azul oscuro** *dark blue*
ostra (f) *oyster*
otra vez *again*
otro *another; other;* **el otro** *the other one;* **en otro sitio** *somewhere else*

P

padastro (m) *stepfather*
padre (m) *father;* **los padres** *parents*
pagar *to pay;* **pagar al contado** *to pay cash*

página (f) *page*
pago (m) *payment*
país (m) *country* (state)
pájaro (m) *bird*
pala (f) *spade*
palabra (f) *word*
palacio (m) *palace*
palanca de velocidades (f) *gear stick*
pálido *pale*
pan (m) *bread*
panadería (f) *bakery*
pañal (m) *nappy;* **los pañales desechables** *disposable nappies*
paño de cocina (m) *dish cloth*
pantalla (f) *lampshade, screen*
pantalón (m) *trousers;* **los pantalones cortos** *shorts*
pantis (m pl) *tights*
pañuelo (m) *headscarf;* **los pañuelos de papel** *tissues*
papá (m) *dad*
papel (m) *paper;* **el papel de envolver/regalo** *wrapping paper;* **el papel de escribir** *writing paper;* **el papel higiénico** *toilet paper;* **los papeles de filtro** *filter papers*
paquete (m) *package, packet, parcel*
par (m) *pair*
para *for;* **es para mí** *it's for me;* **para el viernes** *by Friday;* **¿para qué?** *what for?;* **para una semana** *for a week*
parabrisas (m) *windscreen*
parachoques (m) *bumper*
parada (f) *stop* (bus); **la parada de taxis** *taxi rank*
parafina (f) *paraffin*
paraguas (m) *umbrella*
parar *to stop*
pared (f) *wall* (inside)
pariente (m) *relative*
parque (m) *park*
parrilla (f) *grill*
parte de atrás (f) *back* (not front)
parterre (m) *flowerbed*
partido (m) *match* (sport); *party* (political)
pasajero (m) *passenger*
pasaporte (m) *passport;* **el pasaporte de animales** *pet passport*
pasas (f pl) *raisins*
paseo (m) *walk, stroll;* **ir de paseo** *to go for a walk*

pasillo (m) *aisle, corridor*
paso elevado (m) *flyover*
pasta (f) *pasta*
pasta dentífrica (f) *toothpaste*
pastel (m) *cake* (small)
pastelería (f) *cake shop*
pastilla (f) *pill, tablet;* **las pastillas de menta** *peppermints;* **las pastillas para la garganta** *cough drops*
patata (f) *potato;* **las patatas fritas** *chips, crisps*
patinar *to skid*
patines para hielo (m pl) *ice skates*
peatón (m) *pedestrian*
pecho (m) *chest* (part of body)
pedazo (m) *piece*
pedido (m) *order*
pegamento (m) *adhesive, glue*
peinar *to comb*
peine (m) *comb*
película (f) *film, movie;* **la película en color** *colour film*
peligroso *dangerous*
pelo (m) *hair*
pelota (f) *ball*
peluquería (f) *hairdresser;* **la peluquería de caballeros** *barber*
pendientes (m pl) *earrings*
pensar *to think;* **lo pensaré** *I'll think about it*
pensión completa *full board*
peor *worse, worst*
pepino (m) *cucumber*
pequeño *little, small*
pera (f) *pear*
percha (f) *coat hanger*
¡perdón! *sorry!, excuse me!* (when sneezing etc)
perejil (m) *parsley*
perezoso *lazy*
perfecto *perfect*
perfume (m) *perfume*
periódico (m) *newspaper*
perla (f) *pearl*
permanente (f) *perm*
permiso (m) *licence*
pero *but*
perro (m) *dog*
persianas (f pl) *blinds*
pesado *heavy*
pesca (f) *fishing*
pescadería (f) *fishmonger's*
pescado (m) *fish* (food)
pescar: ir a pescar *to go fishing*

pez (m) *fish* (animal)
piano (m) *piano*
picadura (f) *bite* (by insect)
picaporte (m) *handle* (door)
picar *to bite* (insect)
picas (f pl) *spades* (cards)
picnic (m) *picnic*
pie (m) *foot*
pierna (f) *leg*
pijama (m) *pyjamas*
pila (f) *battery* (torch etc)
piloto (m) *pilot*
pimienta (f) *pepper* (spice)
pimiento (m) *pepper* (red, green)
pin (m) *PIN*
piña (f) *pineapple*
pinchazo (m) *puncture*
pino (m) *pine* (tree)
pintor (m) *decorator*
pintura (f) *paint*
pinza (f) *peg;* **las pinzas** *tweezers*
pipa (f) *pipe* (for smoking)
Pirineos: los Pirineos *Pyrenees*
piscina (f) *swimming pool;* **la piscina municipal** *public swimming pool*
piso (m) *apartment; floor* (storey)
pista (f) *runway*
pistola (f) *gun* (pistol)
piston (m) *piston*
pizza (f) *pizza*
plancha (f) *iron* (for clothes); **a la plancha** *grilled*
planchar *to iron*
plano (m) *town map, town plan;* (adj) *flat, level*
planta (f) *plant*
planta baja (f) *ground floor*
plástico (m) *plastic;* **el plástico para envolver** *plastic wrap*
plata (f) *silver* (metal)
plátano (m) *banana*
plateado *silver* (colour)
platillo (m) *saucer*
plato (m) *plate;* **el plato principal** *main course;* **los platos preparados** *ready meals*
playa (f) *beach*
plaza (f) *pitch, square* (in town); **la plaza de toros** *bullring*
pluma (f) *pen;* **la pluma estilográfica** *fountain pen*
pobre *poor* (not rich)

poco *a little;* **poco común** *unusual;* **poco hecho/pasado** *rare (steak)*
poder *to be able*
policía (f) *police*
policía (m) *police officer*
política (f) *politics*
pollo (m) *chicken*
polvo (m) *powder;* **los polvos** *make-up powder;* **los polvos de talco** *talcum powder*
pomada (f) *ointment*
poner *to put;* **¿me pone ...? can I have ...?**
poquito *a little;* **sólo un poquito** *just a little*
por *through, by, per;* **por avión** *by air mail;* **por la noche** *at night;* **por noche** *per night;* **por todas partes** *everywhere*
porcelana (f) *china (wear)*
por favor *please*
¿por qué? *why?*
porque *because*
portero (m) *caretaker*
Portugal *Portugal*
portugués *Portuguese*
posible *possible*
postal (f) *postcard*
póster (m) *poster*
postigo (m) *shutter (window)*
postre (m) *dessert*
precio (m) *price;* **el precio de entrada** (m) *admission charge*
precioso *beautiful (object)*
preferir *to prefer*
pregunta (f) *question*
presupuesto (m) *budget, estimate*
primavera (f) *spring (season)*
primer piso (m) *first floor*
primero *first;* **de primera** *first class;* **primeros auxilios** *first aid*
primo (m) *cousin*
prima (f) *cousin*
principiante (m/f) *beginner*
principio (m) *start, beginning*
prisa: tengo prisa *I'm in a hurry*
privado *private*
problema (m) *problem*
producto (m) *product;* **los productos de belleza** *beauty products;* **los productos del hogar** *household products;* **los productos lácteos** *dairy products*

profesión (f) *profession*
profesor/profesora (m/f) *teacher*
profesor/profesora de universidad (m/f) *lecturer (university)*
profundo *deep*
programa (m) *schedule*
prohibido *prohibited*
prometida (f) *fiancée*
prometido (m) *fiancé*
prometido/prometida (m/f) *engaged (to be married)*
propina (f) *tip (money)*
próximo *next*
prudente *careful*
prueba (f) *test*
público *public*
pueblo (m) *small town, village*
¿puede ...? *can you ...?*
puedo *I can;* **no puedo** *I can't*
puente (m) *bridge*
puerta (f) *door, gate;* **la puerta de embarque** *departure gate*
puerto (m) *harbour, port*
pulga (f) *flea*
pulpo (m) *octopus*
pulsera (f) *bracelet*
punta (f) *tip (end)*
puro (m) *cigar*

Q

que *than*
¿qué? *what?*
quemadura (f) *burn*
quemadura de sol (f) *sunburn*
quemar *to burn*
querer *to want, love*
querido *dear (person)*
queso (m) *cheese*
¿qué tal? *how are you?*
¿quién? *who?*
quince *fifteen*
quirófano (m) *operating theatre*
quisquillas (f pl) *shrimps*
quizás *maybe, perhaps*

R

rábano (m) *radish*
radiador (m) *radiator*
radio (f) *radio*
rápido *fast, quick*
raro *rare (uncommon)*
rastrillo (m) *rake*
rata (f) *rat*
ratón (m) *mouse*

raya (f) *parting (hair)*
rebajas (f pl) *sale (at reduced prices)*
rebeca (f) *cardigan*
recado (m) *message*
recepción (f) *reception*
recepcionista (m/f) *receptionist*
receta (f) *prescription*
recibo (m) *receipt*
recobrar algo *to get something back*
recogida (f) *collection (postal)*
récord (m) *record (sport etc)*
recuerdo (m) *souvenir*
redondo *round (circular)*
regalo (m) *gift;* **el regalo de cumpleaños** *birthday present*
regla (f) *ruler (for measuring)*
reír *to laugh*
rejilla de equipajes (f) *luggage rack*
relajarse *to relax*
religión (f) *religion*
relleno (m) *filling (in sandwich, cake)*
reloj (m) *clock, watch*
remar *to row*
remolque (m) *trailer*
remos (m pl) *oars*
resaca (f) *hangover*
reserva (f) *reservation*
reservar *to book*
resfriado (m) *cold (illness);* **tengo un resfriado** *I have a cold*
respirar *to breathe*
restaurante (m) *restaurant*
resto (m) *rest, remainder*
retrasado *delayed;* **el autobús se ha retrasado** *the bus is late*
reunión (f) *meeting*
revelar *to develop (film)*
revista (f) *magazine*
rico *rich*
rímel (m) *mascara*
rincón (m) *corner (of room)*
riñón (m) *kidney*
río (m) *river*
rizos (m pl) *curls*
robar *steal;* **lo han robado** *it's been stolen*
robo (m) *robbery*
roca (f) *rock (stone)*
rock (m) *rock (music)*
rodilla (f) *knee*
rojo *red*
ron (m) *rum*

ropa (f) *clothes*; **la ropa de cama** (f) *bed linen*; **la ropa interior** *underwear*; **la ropa sucia** *laundry (dirty)*
rosa (adj) *pink*
rosa (f) *rose*
roto *broken*
rotonda (f) *roundabout*
rotulador (m) *felt-tip pen*
roulotte (f) *caravan*
rubí (m) *ruby (stone)*
rubio *blond(e) (adj)*
rueda (f) *wheel*; **la rueda pinchada** *flat tyre*
rugby (m) *rugby*
ruidoso *noisy*
ruinas (f pl) *ruins*
rulos (m pl) *curlers*

S

sábado *Saturday*
sábana (f) *sheet (bedding)*
saber *to know (fact)*; **no sé** *I don't know*
sabor (m) *flavour*
sacacorchos (m) *corkscrew*
sacapuntas (m) *pencil sharpener*
sacar *to bring out*
saco de dormir (m) *sleeping bag*
sal (f) *salt*
sala de espera (f) *waiting room*
sala de pediatría (f) *children's ward*
salchicha (f) *sausage*
salida (f) *exit, departure*; **las salidas** *departures*; **la salida de emergencia** *emergency exit*
salmón (m) *salmon*
salón (m) *lounge (in hotel)*
salsa (f) *sauce*
¡salud! *cheers! (toast)*
sandalias (f pl) *sandals*
sangre (f) *blood*
sartén (f) *frying pan*
sauna (f) *sauna*
secador (de pelo) (m) *hairdryer*
seco *dry*
sed *thirsty*; **tengo sed** *I'm thirsty*
seda (f) *silk*
segundo (m) *second (noun; adj)*; **de segunda** *second class*
seguro (m) *insurance*; (adj) *sure, safe (not dangerous)*
seis *six*

sello (m) *stamp*
selva *rainforest*
semáforo (m) *traffic lights*
semana (f) *week*; **la semana pasada** *last week*; **la semana que viene** *next week*
seminario (m) *seminar*
semi-seco *medium-dry (wine)*
señal (f) *deposit*
sencillo *simple*
senderismo (m) *hiking*
señor *Mr, sir*
señora *Mrs, madam*
señorita *Miss*
separado *separated*
septiembre *September*
ser *to be*
serio *serious*
seropositivo *HIV positive*
servicio (m) *service, department*; **el servicio de habitaciones** *room service*; **el servicio de radiología** *x-ray department*; **el servicio de urgencias** *emergency department*
servicios (m pl) *toilets (in public establishment)*; **los servicios de caballeros** *men's toilets*; **los servicios de señoras** *women's toilets*
servilleta (f) *napkin*
sesenta *sixty*
setas (f pl) *mushrooms*
setenta *seventy*
seto (m) *hedge*
si *if, whether*
sí *yes*
Sida (m) *AIDS*
siempre *always*
siete *seven*
significar: ¿qué significa esto? *what does this mean?*
siguiente *next*
silla (f) *chair*; **la silla de ruedas** *wheelchair*
sillita de ruedas (f) *stroller, pushchair*
simpático *friendly*
sin *without*; **sin plomo** *unleaded*
sinagoga (f) *synagogue*
sitio (m) *room, space*; **el sitio web** *website*
sobre (m) *envelope*
sobre todo *especially*
sobrina (f) *niece*
sobrino (m) *nephew*
soda (f) *soda water*

sofa (m) *sofa*
sofocante *close, stuffy*
sol (m) *sun*
solo *alone*; **yo solo** *by myself*
sólo *just, only*
soltero/soltera (m/f) *single (unmarried)*
sombrero (m) *hat*
sombrilla (f) *sunshade*
somnífero (m) *sleeping pill*
somos *we are*
son *they are*
sonreír *to smile*
sonrisa (f) *smile*
sopa (f) *soup*
sordo *deaf*
sostén (m) *bra*
sótano (m) *basement*
soy *I am*; **soy de ...** *I come from ...*
spray (m) *inhaler (for asthma etc)*; **el spray antipulgas** *flea spray*
su (s) *its/hers/his/your (formal)*; **¿es suyo esto?** *is this yours?*
subirse *to get in, get on (of train, bus etc)*
sucio *dirty*
sudadera (f) *sweatshirt*
Sudamérica *South America*
sudar *to sweat*
sudor (m) *sweat*
suelo (m) *floor*; **el suelo aislante** *groundsheet*
sueño (m) *sleep*
suerte (f) *luck*; **¡suerte!** *good luck!*
supermercado (m) *supermarket*
suplemento (m) *supplement*
supositorio (m) *suppository*
sur (m) *south*

T

tabaco (m) *tobacco*
tabla de windsurfing (f) *sailboard*
tableta de chocolate (f) *bar of chocolate*
tacón (m) *heel (shoe)*
taller (m) *garage (for repairs)*
talón (m) *heel (foot)*
talonario de cheques (m) *chequebook*
también *too (also)*
tampones (m pl) *tampons*

tan *so*; **tan bueno** *so good*

tanto: **no tanto** *not so much*; **tanto … como …** *both … and …*

tapiz (m) *tapestry*

tapón (m) *cap* (bottle), *plug* (sink)

taquilla (f) *box office, ticket office*

tarde (f) *evening*; (adj) *late*; *it's getting late* **se está haciendo** *tarde*

tarifa (f) *fare*

tarjeta (f) *card*; **la tarjeta de banco** *bank card*; **la tarjeta de crédito** *credit card*; **la tarjeta de embarque** *boarding pass*; **la tarjeta de vista** *business card*; **la tarjeta telefónica** *phonecard*

tarta (f) *cake* (large)

taxi (m) *taxi*

taza (f) *cup*

té (m) *tea*

techo (m) *ceiling*

teclado (m) *keyboard*

técnico (m) *technician*

tejado (m) *roof*

tejanos (m pl) *jeans*

tela (f) *material* (cloth)

teleférico (m) *cable car*

teléfono (m) *telephone*; **el teléfono móvil** *mobile phone*

televisión (f) *television*; **la television por** *cable cable TV*

temperatura (f) *temperature*

temprano *early*

tenedor (m) *fork*

tener *to have*; **tengo** *I have*; **no tengo** *I don't have*; **¿tiene?** *do you have?*; **tengo que irme** *I have to go*; **tengo calor** *I feel hot*; **tengo que …** *I must …*

teñir *to bleach* (hair)

tenis (m) *tennis*

tenue *faint* (unclear)

tercero *third*

terminal (f) *terminal*

ternera (f) *veal*

terraza (f) *terrace*

testigo (m) *witness*

tía (f) *aunt*

tiempo (m) *time, weather*

tienda (f) *shop*; **la tienda de comestibles** *grocer's*; **la tienda de discos** *record store*

tienda (de campaña) (f) *tent*

¿tiene …? *do you have …?*

tierra (f) *land, soil*

tijeras (f pl) *scissors*

timbre (m) *bell* (door)

tinta (f) *ink*

tinto *red* (wine)

tintorería (f) *dry cleaner*

tío (m) *uncle*

tirantes (m pl) *braces*

tirar de *to pull*

tirita (f) *plaster*

toalla (f) *towel*

toallitas para bebé (f pl) *baby wipes*

tobillo (m) *ankle*

toca: **me toca a mí** *it's my turn*

tocadiscos (m) *record player*

tocar *to feel* (touch)

todavía *yet*; **todavía no** *not yet*

todo *everything, all*; **eso es todo** *that's all*

todos *everyone*

todos los días *every day*

tomar *to take*; **tomar el sol** *to sunbathe*

tomate (m) *tomato*

tónica (f) *tonic*

torero (m) *bullfighter*

tormenta (f) *storm*

tornillo (m) *screw*

toro (m) *bull*

torre (f) *tower*

tortilla (f) *omelette*

tos (f) *cough*

toser *to cough*

tostada (f) *toast*

trabajar *to work* (job)

trabajo (m) *job, work*

tractor (m) *tractor*

tradición (f) *tradition*

traducir *to translate*

traductor/traductora (m/f) *translator*

traer *to fetch*

tráfico (m) *traffic*

traje (m) *suit* (clothing)

tranquilo *quiet*

trapo del polvo (m) *duster*

trasero (m) *bottom* (part of body)

tréboles (m pl) *clubs* (cards)

trece *thirteen*

treinta *thirty*

tren (m) *train*

tres *three*

triste *sad*

tú *you* (informal)

tu (s) *your* (informal); **tu libro** *your book*; **tus zapatos** *your shoes*; **¿es tuyo esto?** *is this yours?*

tubería (f) *pipe* (for water)

tubo de escape (m) *exhaust*

tuerca (f) *nut* (for bolt)

tuerza (**a la izquierda/derecha**) *turn* (left/right)

túnel (m) *tunnel*

turismo (m) *sightseeing*

turista (m/f) *tourist*

U

último *last* (final)

ultramarinos (m) *grocer*

un/una *a*

uña (f) *finger nail*

único *single* (only)

universidad (f) *university*

uno *one*

urgente *urgent*

usar *to use*

uso (m) *use*

usted *you* (formal)

utensilios de cocina (m pl) *cooking utensils*

útil *useful*

uvas (f pl) *grapes*

V

vacaciones (f pl) *holiday*

vacío *empty*

vacuna (f) *vaccination*

vagón (m) *carriage* (train); **el vagón-restaurante** *restaurant car*

vainilla (f) *vanilla*

vale *OK*

valle (m) *valley*

válvula (f) *valve*

vapor (m) *steam, steamer* (boat); **al vapor** *steamed*

vaqueros (m pl) *jeans*

varios *several*

vaso (m) *glass* (for drinking)

váter (m) *toilet* (item in bathroom)

¡váyase! *go away!*

veces: **a veces** *sometimes*

vegetariano *vegetarian*

vehículo (m) *vehicle*

veinte *twenty*

vela (f) *sailing; candle*

velocidad (f) *speed*

venda (f) *bandage*

vender to sell
veneno (m) poison
venir to vome; **¡venga aquí!**
  come here!
ventana (f) window
ventas (f pl) sales
ventilador (m) fan
  (ventilator)
ventisca (f) blizzard
ver to see; **no veo** I
  can't see
verdad true; **es verdad** it's
  true; **¿verdad?** isn't that so?
verde green
verdulería (f) greengrocer's
verdura (f) vegetables
verja (f) gate
vestido (m) dress
veterinario (m) vet
vez: de vez en cuando
  occasionally
viajar to travel; **viajar en**
  avión fly (of person)
viaje (m) journey;
el viaje de novios
  honeymoon
vida (f) life
vídeo (m) video (film); **el**
  (aparato de) **vídeo** video
  recorder
videocámara (f) camcorder
vídeo-juegos (m pl)
  computer/video games
viejo old
viento (m) wind
viernes Friday
vigilante nocturno (m)
  night porter
vinagre (m) vinegar
vinatero (m) wine merchant
vino (m) wine
violín (m) violin
visita (f) visit; **las horas de**
  visita visiting hours; **la visita**
  con guía guided tour
visitante (m/f) visitor
visitar to visit
visor de imagen (m)
viewfinder
vista (f) view
vitaminas (f pl) vitamin
  pills
vivero (m) garden centre
vodka (m) vodka
volar to fly (plane, insect)
volver to come/get back,
return; **nos volvemos**
mañana we get back
tomorrow
voz (f) voice
vuelo (m) flight

W, Y, Z

web site (f) website
whisky (m) whisky
y and
ya already
yo I
yogur (m) yoghurt
zanahoria (f) carrot
zapatería (f) shoe shop
zapatilla (f) washing machine
zapatillas (f pl) slippers
zapatos (m pl) shoes; **los**
  zapatos de deporte
  trainers
zona peatonal (f) pedestrian
  zone
zoo (m) zoo
zumo juice (m); **el zumo de**
  frutas fruit juice; **el zumo**
  de naranja orange juice;
  el zumo de tomate
  tomato juice

Acknowledgments

The publisher would like to thank the following for their help: Isa Palacios and Maria Serna for the organization of location photography in Spain; Restaurant Raymon at Mi Pueblo, Madrid; Magnet Showroom, Enfield, London; MyHotel, London; Peppermint Green Hairdressers, London; Coolhurst Tennis Club, London; Kathy Gammon; Juliette Meeus and Harry.

Language content for Dorling Kindersley by **g-and-w publishing**
Managed by **Jane Wightwick**
Editing and additional input: **Cathy Gaulter-Carter, Teresa Cervera, Leila Gaafar**

Additional design assistance: **Phil Gamble, Lee Riches, Fehmi Cömert, Sally Geeve**
Additional editorial assistance: **Kajal Mistry, Paul Docherty, Lynn Bresler**
Picture research: **Louise Thomas**

Picture credits

Key: t=top; b=bottom; l=left; r=right; c=centre; A=above; B=below

p2 **DK Images**: *Joan Farre*; p4/5 **Alamy**: *Image Source tl*; **Alamy**:*D Hurst bl*; *Indiapicture bcl*; p10/11 **Alamy**: *BananaStock cAr*; **Getty**: *Taxi / James Day cBl*; **Ingram Image Library**: *bl*; p12/13 **Alamy**: *Dynamics Graphics Group / Creatas cBr*; *John Foxx cAr*; *RubberBall br*; **DK Images**: *cl*; **Ingram Image Library**: *tl, cr*; p14/15 **DK Images**: *tcr*; **Dreamstime.com**: *Slobodan Mračina (cl)*; **Ingram Image Library**: *cl, cBl, cAr, cBr, bcr*; p16/17 **Getty**: *Taxi / James Day bcr*; **Ingram Image LiBrary**: *tr*; p18/19 **DK Images**: *David Murray tr*; p22/23 **DK Images**: *cl, Andy Crawford cAr*; *Susanna Price br*; *Magnus Rew tcrB*; **Ingram Image Library**: *tcr*; p24/25 **DK Images**: *clA, Dave King tcr*; p26/27 **Alamy**: *Dynamic Graphics Group / Creatas cl*; p28/29 **DK Images**: *John Bulmer tcr*; *Dave King cr*; *Matthew Ward bclA*; **Ingram Image Library**: *bcrA, bcr*; p30/31 **Alamy**: *Comstock Images bcl* *Think Stock bclA*; **DK Images**: *cl*; p34/35 **Dreamstime.com**: *Slobodan Mračina (cb)*; **Ingram Image Library**: *tcr*; **iStockphoto.com**: *nicolas_ (tl)*; p36/37 **DK Images**: *bcl, bcr*; *Magnus Rew cl*; **Dreamstime.com**: *Slobodan Mračina (cla)*; **Ingram Image Library**: *bl*; **iStockphoto.com**: *nicolas_ (cla/sim card)*; p38/39 **Alamy**: *Imageshop / Zefa Visual Media cl*; **Ingram Image Library**: *cr*; p40/41 **DK Images**: *Peter Wilson bl*; **Lee Riches**: *cl*; p42/43 **Alamy**: *Image Source tcr, cAr, cAAr*; p44/45 **Alamy**: *Jon Arnold Images br*; *ImageState / Ethel Davies bl*; *Vikki Martin cbl*; *Peter Titmuss bcrr*; **Alamy**: *Iain Davidson Photographic bcll*; *David O'Shea bcr*; *Courtesy of Renault*: *c*; p46/47 **Alamy**: *Imageshop / Zefa Visual Media br*; **Ingram Image Library**: *cr*; *Courtesy of Renault*: *tcrB*; **Lee Riches**: *bcl*; p48/49 **Alamy**: *Balearic Pictures c*; **Alamy**: *Brand X Pictures bcl*; **DK Images**: *tcr, bcl*; *Neil Lukas bcr*; *John Miller crA*; **Lee Riches**: *cl*; p50/51 **Alamy**: *Peter Titmuss cr*; **Lee Riches**: *c*; p52/53 **Alamy**: *Jean Dominique Dallet tcr*; **Alamy**: *Image Farm Inc cAr*; *Imageshop - Zefa Visual Media tcrB*; **DK Images**: *cl*; p54/55 **Alamy**: *Jackson Smith cBl*; **Alamy**: *Brand X Pictures cl*; *John Foxx c*; *Image Source cAr*; *ThinkStock tcr*; **DK Images**: *Andy Crawford bcl*; p56/57 **Alamy**: *Balearic Pictures clA*; **Alamy**: *Brand X Pictures clAA*; **DK Images**: *cl*; *Neil Lukas tl*; *John Miller tcll*; **Lee Riches**: *tcl*; *Courtesy of Renault*: *bc*; p58/59 **Alamy**: *Michael Juno tcr*; **Alamy**: *Brand X Pictures cBl, cBBl*; *Ingram Publishing cAAl*; **DK Images**: *cAl*; *Max Alexander cBr*; p60/61 **123RF.com**: *shutswis (cb)*; **Alamy**: *Robert Harding Picture Library bcr*; **Alamy**: *Image Source cAr*; **DK Images**: *Steve Gorton bl, tcrB*; *Pia Tryde cAAr*; **Ingram Image Library**: *cr*; p62/63 **DK Images**: *Stephen Whitehorn c*; p64/65 **Alamy**: *Arcaid bcrA*; *Mike Kipling c*; **Alamy**: *GKPhotography cBr*; *Goodshoot cAAr*; *Justin Kase tcrB*; **DK Images**: *Steve Tanner cAr*; **Ingram Image Library**: *tcr*; p66/67 **Alamy**: *Arcaid tl*; **Alamy**: *Ingram Publishing cAr*; **DK Images**: *tr*; *Stephen Whitehorn bl*; **Ingram Image Library**: *cAr*; p68/69 **Alamy**: *Balearic Pictures cr*; *directphoto.org cAr*; *Doug Houghton cl*; *Indiapicture clB*; **Alamy**: *CoverSpot cBl*; **Lee Riches**: *cBr*; p72/73 **Alamy**: *imagebroker tcrB*; *Image Source cAr*; *Comstock Images tcr*; **Avery Weight-Tronix**: *bl*; p74/75 **Alamy RF**: *Doug Norman bl*; **Ingram Image Library**: *c*; p76/77 **Alamy**: *Balearic Pictures cBl*; *Indiapicture bl*; **Alamy**: *Coverspot clB*; p78/79 **Alamy**: *Luca DiCecco bcl*; *Steve Hamblin bcr*; p80/81 **Getty**: *Taxi / Rob Melnychuk bc*; **Ingram Image Library**: *cAr*; *Xerox UK Ltd*: *tcr*; p82/83 **Alamy**: *wildphotos.com tcr*; **Alamy**: *FogStock cAAl*; *Momentum Creative Group cAl*; *Shoosh / Up the Res cBl*; **Ingram Image Library**: *cl*; p84/85 **Alamy**: *Brand X Pictures cr*; *f1* **Alamy RF**: *BananaStock bl*; *Comstock Images c*; *SuperStock tr*; **Ingram Image Library**: *crB*; p86/87 **Alamy**: *Luca DiCecco bcl*; **Getty**: *Taxi / Rob Melnychuk tc*; p90/91 **Alamy**: *Brand X Pictures tcr*; **DK Images**: *cl*; *David Jordan cAr*; *Stephen Oliver cr*; **Ingram Image Library**: *cBr*; p82/93 **Alamy**: *Pixland cr*; **DK Images**: *cl*; *Guy Ryecart tr*; p94/95 **Alamy**: *David Kamm cl*; *Phototake Inc bcl*; **Alamy**: *Comstock Images cr*; *ImageState Royalty Free bcr*; **DK Images**: *Stephen Oliver tcr*; p96/97 **Alamy**: *Pixland br*; **DK Images**: *tl*; **Ingram Image Library**: *tr*; p98/99 **Alamy**: *Andrew Linscott c*; *Shotfile cr*; **Alamy**: *Bildagentur Franz Waldhaeusl bl*; *ThinkStock br*; **Dreamstime.com**: *Alexandre Dvihally (tl)*; p100/101 **DK Images**: *Steve Gorton tcr*; p102/103 **Alamy**: *Hortus b*; *D Hurst tcrB*; **Alamy**: *image100 tcr*; *Barry Mason cAAr*; **Ingram Image Library**: *cAr*; p104/105 **DK Images**: *Paul Bricknell cl(6)*; *Jane Burton bcl*; *Geoff Dann cl(2)*; *Max Gibbs cl(4)*; *Frank Greenaway cl(3)*; *Dave King cl(1), cAr*; *Tracy Morgan cl(5)*; p106/107 **Alamy**: *Shotfile cr*; **Alamy**: *Barry Mason br*; p110/111 **Alamy**: *Think Stock cAr*; **DK Images**: *Andy Crawford cl*; p112/113 **Alamy RF**: *Dynamic Graphics Group / Creatas tcr*; *image100 bl*; **Ingram Image Library**: *cl; bcrA*; p114/115 **Alamy**: *John Cole cr*; **Alamy**: *Image Source cAr*; *Index Stock cAl*; *jackhollingsworth.com tcr*; p116/117 **Alamy**: *Dynamics Graphics Group / Creatas clA*; *John Foxx clB*; p118/119 **Alamy**: *D Hurst c*; **Alamy**: *Pixland tcr*; p120/121 **Alamy**: *ImageState / Pictor International cl*; **Alamy**: *Shotfile cBl*; **Alamy**: *Sarkis Images tcr*; **DK Images**: *bcl*; p122/123 **Alamy**: *BananaStock cA*; **Ingram Image Library**: *cl*; p124/125 **Alamy**: *ImageState / Pictor International bclA*; *Shotfile cBl*; **DK Images**: *bcl*; *Paul Bricknell tc(5)*; *Geoff Dann tc(3)*; *Max Gibbs tc(1)*; *Frank Greenaway tc(2)*; *Dave King tc(4)*; *Tracy Morgan tc(6)*; **Ingram Image Library**: *bl*; p126/127 **Alamy**: *Jean Dominique Dallet clB*; **Alamy**: *Imageshop - Zefa Visual Media blA*; *Image Farm Inc bl*; p128 **DK Images**.

All other images **Mike Good.***